PRAYER BOOTCAMP

PREPARATION FOR THE BATTLE OF YOUR LIFE

BOOK ONE

An Interactive & Experiential Prayer Discipleship Workbook

HIDDEN MANNA MINISTRY

WHITESTONE PUBLISHING
2011

Whitestone Publishing
P. O. Box 928
Somis, California 93066
USA
www.hiddenmannaministry.com

Prayer Boot Camp – Preparation for the Battle of Your Life

Requests for information regarding Hidden Manna Ministry should be addressed to:
Hidden Manna Ministry
P. O. Box 928
Somis, California 93066 USA
www.hiddenmannaministry.com

ISBN 987-0-615-44481-9

With Gratitude and Appreciation

Hidden Manna Ministry is grateful to so many friends and fellow travelers in the journey to complete *Prayer Boot Camp*. We are especially indebted to the enthusiastic efforts and engagement of the many disciples willing to 'test drive' these units as soon as we finished them. Among them, the Calvary Chapel Skyline Prayer Group and several test teams from Evangelical Free Church of the Conejo Valley who took up these units two and three times to help render an effective and free-flowing curriculum. Thank you for standing with us through many months of writing and revisioning.

This project has opened doors of partnership with people across the country with similar hearts and hunger for more of Jesus. Disciples like Jennifer Jones, whose extraordinary artwork (including the *Warrior's Sword* on our cover) is touching the lives of so many and inviting them into deeper fellowship with Jesus (gloryglimpses.blogspot. com). She seems like one of our team and her inspiration has been a defining grace to us. And closer to home, Joel Hickenbottom, a gifted disciple whose talent and vision have helped translate *Prayer Boot Camp* to a dynamic 'dunamis' workbook experience with Jesus.

We are also indebted to Tree of Life Fellowship who shared their God-blessed hilltop home with Hidden Manna and provided covering and encouragement through many years of ministry.

Our gratitude would not be complete without acknowledging Community Bible Study/Camarillo for many years of building into the spiritual foundation of what has become Hidden Manna Ministry. Your passion and dedication to the Word of God and the Body of Christ in our region have helped to shape our faith and ministry. Special thanks to Margaret Frost for her unrelenting love and confidence in our quest for a deeper experience of the Word on behalf of the faith community.

We could not have finished *Prayer Boot Camp* without the partnership, prayer cover and patient endurance of our husbands who have supported this dream and vision from the outset, often at considerable sacrifice to themselves. Our travail and deliberation have taken many hours that could well have been spent in ways that might have seemed of greater value to lesser men. But not to these men, who love us out of deep God-filled wells of grace.

Without the active support of so many of you, we would not be launching *Prayer Boot Camp* today. We are thankful for Christ in each one who has hungered with us and labored alongside so that the Body of Christ may be built up into "the whole measure of the fullness of Christ."

And most of all, we are grateful to our Shepherd-King who has guided us through sometimes treacherous terrain until He brings us to the green pastures and still waters of that sweet place in His presence. The experience of writing *Prayer Boot Camp* has been like a mysterious dance—the Spirit leading us through steps of His Word as we follow with the declarations of our hearts in response to Him. Father, thank you for your unfailing love and faithfulness. We celebrate the privilege of this dance with you—a romance and a war dance, all in one.

HIDDEN MANNA MINISTRY TEAM
Toni Behrend, Patti Goldberg, Dana Tibbitts, Celeste Malmo, Donna Bolding, Kerry Azbell

WELCOME

Hidden Manna Ministry – "What is it?"

No, really. That is the meaning of "manna." When the Father provided astonishing little flakes of bread from heaven to His people wandering in the Sinai desert, that's what they called it. "Manna. *What is it?*" Today, Hidden Manna Ministry is an expression of the Father's longing to nurture His people and bring them to the feet of Jesus for refreshment and transformation . . . the 'daily bread' of His Word and Holy Spirit.

Hidden Manna Ministry is a place of prayer and provision for the journey in Jesus Christ. Our ministry team offers discipleship resources, training, prayer and pastoral care in the Southern California area. Our passion is to serve the Lord and seek His transforming power for His church through worship, prayer and the sword of the Word. Hidden Manna is all about building unity, community and intimacy with Jesus. We offer spiritual retreats and refreshment, prayer ministry and healing, as well as an array of discipleship resources.

Our team, which represents a variety of churches, served together in Community Bible Study for more than a decade before forming Hidden Manna Ministry in 2002. Since then we have grown in ministry to God's people, outreach to the Body of Christ, and absolute reliance on the Holy Spirit.

For some time, the Father had been nudging us to put to paper the things He has been teaching us for the last 15 years or more about prayer—personal, corporate, ministry and caring prayer. It has been a journey to grow in our intimacy, identity and authority in Jesus. The job of trying to explain what we are still learning seemed daunting. But as we stepped out in obedience, the Lord has been faithful to our process of sifting and sorting, honing and distilling, culling and refining until we have *Prayer Boot Camp*.

Even now, we take it up with a measure of astonishment. How did this possibly come from such an ungainly process? We can only conclude and declare—may it be less of us and more of Him! He has been so faithful and patient to redeem our best efforts to create something that, even to us, feels fresh and alive when we return to it.

What we Believe
We believe in Jesus Christ, God's only begotten Son incarnate, who died for our sins that we might receive life—both abundant and eternal (John 3:16; 10:10). He was resurrected from the dead and sits at the right hand of God where, even now, He intercedes for us (Romans 8:34). The Bible is the infallible Word of God (2 Timothy 3:16). We are called and empowered through the Holy Spirit to do the same things Christ did in accordance with His truth and love (John 14:12-14).

Now we entrust the Holy Spirit to guide and bless each of you through your own journey with *Prayer Boot Camp*. Allow the Spirit to mentor you and minister to you in ways you never imagined possible!

In the Love of Christ,

HIDDEN MANNA MINISTRY TEAM
Toni Behrend, Patti Goldberg, Dana Tibbitts, Celeste Malmo, Donna Bolding, Kerry Azbell

TABLE OF CONTENTS

units

PRAYER
BOOTCAMP

PREPARATION FOR THE BATTLE OF YOUR LIFE

PRAYER BOOT CAMP BASIC TRAINING

"Our prayer is that you—being rooted and established in love—may have power together with all the saints to grasp how wide and long and high and deep is the love of Christ, and to know this love that surpasses knowledge, that you may be filled to the measure of all the fullness of God. . . . It was he who gave some to be apostles, some to be prophets, some to be evangelists, and some to be pastors and teachers, to prepare God's people for works of service, so that the body of Christ may be built up until we all reach unity in the faith and in the knowledge of the Son of God and become mature, attaining to the whole measure of the fullness of Christ." (Ephesians 3:17-18; 4:11-13)

Prayer Boot Camp is not a book **about** prayer as much as an instrument of engagement **with** prayer to help disciples grow into deeper relationship and spiritual authority in Jesus Christ.

Many Christians—even mature believers—while hearing the admonition to "pray always," find themselves at a loss as to how to sustain such devotion in practice. The danger is that prayer then becomes another list, formula or rule—a drudgery rather than a vibrant experience of adventure and intimacy with Christ. If we are to be salt and light in a broken world, we cannot do so apart from prayer.

This 12-unit basic training offers an arsenal of skills, practices and essential scriptures needed for vigorous and victorious faith in trying times. While both personal and corporate in focus, *Prayer Boot Camp* is designed with groups and communities in mind who desire more dynamic prayer experience and relationship.

Practical Considerations

Prayer Boot Camp is interactive, experiential and relational. It is not meant to be read passively for information to apply to some future prayer experience, but as interaction with the present reality of *the Word that is God, is with God, who became flesh and dwells among us* (John 1:1, 14). As it is read slowly and aloud in community, each unit becomes an interactive discipleship tool that fully engages reader and listener with the Living Word. While *Prayer Boot Camp* may be used on an individual basis, its primary purpose is for use in small group communities of fifteen or fewer members.

The twelve units in *Prayer Boot Camp* are a progressive journey toward a deeper prayer experience with God. Plan for at least twelve group meetings, each dedicated to a single unit. Participants should be instructed to bring a Bible to each session. You may desire to have an additional preliminary meeting to introduce the material, read aloud through introductory notes, and discuss group logistics. An additional closing meeting dedicated to celebration, evaluation and future plans for your group may also be helpful.

Please note there are three optional **Review and Reflect** units. These can be used as additional or supplementary sessions after Unit 4, Unit 8, and Unit 12. They are designed to reinforce the materials presented in the previous units and provide opportunity for further exploration of the prayer experience itself. Should you opt to use **Review and Reflect** as part of the *Prayer Boot Camp* curriculum, you will need to add three additional meeting times to your schedule.

Additional Training Exercises are provided in the event you desire to reinforce a unit's content or to extend your *Prayer Boot Camp* experience by repeating the material in its entirety with fresh **Training** exercises.

Each unit requires about 90 minutes, depending on time allowance for group reflection and discussion. **Training** exercises are included for individual work during group time. Direction is provided at the end of each unit for those seeking ways of **Going Deeper** in their personal time between sessions.

Prayer Boot Camp gives everyone a voice. A voice to read aloud. A voice to reflect and engage in the work of spiritual equipping. It is not about having "right answers" to the **Reflection Questions** or exercises, but experiencing the freedom to express and explore what God is revealing in your journey with Him. If you tend to be uncomfortable praying aloud or speaking out in a group, fear not! While the circle invites each member to read aloud from the workbook, there is no obligation to share your personal reflections unless you wish to.

That said, we pray that this curriculum will free each one of us to a place of fearlessness where we can no longer be intimidated but may receive the fruit of discipleship that God longs to release in each of us as we "attain the whole measure of the fullness of Christ." You will find that the shared fellowship and revelation that comes from other group members will amplify and enrich your own experience of *Prayer Boot Camp*.

As with all tools of discipleship, *Prayer Boot Camp* relies on the active work of the Holy Spirit to instruct and mediate a deeper revelation of Christ to our hearts.

Three Streams of Engagement

Prayer Boot Camp has three streams that run through each unit—**Centrality of Worship**, **Necessity of Stillness**, and **Foundation of Scripture**. These core strategies provide keys to vitality and victory in the battle of our life.

◆ **Worship** – God's original intention was that we walk in intimacy with Him. This is not an intellectual exercise but a deeply emotional reality. Each unit opens with a time of 'listening worship' where we unclutter our minds and refocus our hearts on the person and presence of Jesus Christ. As the first stream in the curriculum, we will discover how worship reorders the spiritual atmosphere, while providing an essential weapon of our warfare.

- **Stillness** – We live in a noisy world. Our tech-heavy culture insists itself on every facet of our being, offering endless distractions and disruptions to our peace. We will learn to contend for our stillness—that yielded interior place that abides in Christ, attuned to the still small voice of God and the cadence of His Spirit working in us.

- **Scripture** – The Word is the creative and re-creative instrument of God's "Kingdom come and will be done" authority in the world. Sharper than any two-edged sword, Scripture is the weapon of choice for wielding His authority in the battlefield of faith. Word-rich and Scripture-steeped, this curriculum is a tool of engagement with the core prayer strategy of the battle-ready warrior.

What is Prayer?

Our view in *Prayer Boot Camp* is that all communion, communication and relationship with God is "prayer." After all, prayer is not simply a few words of thanks spoken over a meal, nor the time we spend in private devotion with the Lord and His Word. In its fullest sense, prayer is the ongoing, unceasing way of being with God through ordinary days and circumstances, sometimes with words, other times with quiet thoughts and subtle interactions in the spirit. With songs, murmurings and quiet contemplation, we begin to forge a more constant orientation to the things of God while being fully present to the people and circumstances around us.

Prayer is the progressive—and ultimately unbroken—expression of our dependence on and delight in our Heavenly Father. A healthy prayer life sows spiritual vitality to our hearts as we increasingly "taste and see" that He is good, and that being in His presence is like nothing else on this earth. This communion is at the heart of the great adventure with God that we call prayer.

What is the battle?

We live in a time of escalating tension between the flesh and the spirit. We are in the world but not of it. Yet, increasingly, believers are subject to conflicting world views and values at odds with our identity in Christ. Unless we establish deep love-roots and vigorous faith in Him who calls us out of darkness and into the light, how can we hope to be salt and light in a hurting world?

The spiritual battle that rages around and within us targets our intimacy, identity and authority in Christ Jesus. It is a battle for our peace and trust in God. It is a battle for our faith and confidence in His promises. Make no mistake—this is a battle for our life.

"Our struggle is not against flesh and blood, but against the rulers, against the authorities, against the powers of this dark world and against the spiritual forces of evil in the heavenly realms." (Ephesians 6:12)

Prayer is the battleground. We must contend for it. It is not a striving in our flesh but a resolve in our spirit to stand fast and fix our eyes on the author and perfecter of our faith—Jesus Christ.

Do we know God in the way He desires to be known?

God invites His children to draw near in covenant relationship through Jesus Christ and the power of His Holy Spirit. Only by the revelation of the Holy Spirit can we know God as He truly wants to be known. Only by His Spirit can we walk in our true identity as the beloved of God. Only by His Spirit can we function in the Kingdom authority of Christ.

For this reason, this workbook is not inductive but experiential. It is a Word-rich encounter that brings us face to face with the Living Word in the battle for our intimacy, identity and authority in Jesus Christ.

Facilitating a Group

Each group session requires approximately 90 minutes. Although you may have a designated leader charged with logistics and communication, *Prayer Boot Camp* is designed to work in a leaderless format. Each week a different person is encouraged to volunteer as Facilitator to guide the group through the next unit and *Training* exercise. No study or preparation is required for the Facilitator other than to read through the unit in advance. Simply follow instructions for facilitating the group and allow the Holy Spirit to use your natural capacity for discipleship.

- ◆ **Opening Prayer** – Open with a short prayer that welcomes the presence of God and invites group members to focus their attention on Him.

- ◆ **Listening Worship** – Allow 5-10 minutes for "listening worship." Each unit comes with a list of *Worship Suggestions*. You may use these recommendations or other songs and hymns conducive to quieting hearts and minds. Close the "listening worship" with a brief prayer asking God for revelation as you journey together through the unit.

- ◆ **Introduction** – Read Unit Introduction to the group.

- ◆ **Strategy** – Ask someone to read the *Strategy* which highlights core principles for each unit.

- ◆ **Read Aloud** – Points and Scriptures are meant to be <u>slowly</u> read aloud. Continue around the circle, taking turns, asking each person to read a point and the Scripture following it. Scripture citations are for reference only. They do not need to be read aloud.

- ◆ **Reflection Question** – At the end of each section are *Reflection Questions* designed to invite conversation concerning the points and Scriptures just read. Read the *Reflection Question* and allow each person a few moments to respond if they choose.

- ◆ **Strategy Recap and For Clarity** – Ask someone to read the *Strategy Recap* and *For Clarity* where included.

- ◆ **Training** – Each unit includes a *Training* exercise. Read the instructions aloud to the group. Allow 10-20 minutes, depending on the directions and available time. At the end of the allotted time, guide the group through the sharing portion of the *Training* exercise.

- ◆ **Going Deeper** – Point out *Going Deeper* exercises designed for use in personal quiet time with God between sessions. Members often benefit from reviewing the unit alone with God.

- ◆ **Facilitator for the Following Week** – Ask for a volunteer to facilitate the group at the next meeting. Kingdom discipleship and multiplication principles invite members to step up and into their God-given identity as disciples of Christ, trusting in the Spirit to guide them. Once members are familiar with the working of the unit, this will not be a daunting role.

- ◆ **Close in Prayer** – Close with a short prayer or The Lord's Prayer. If time permits, pray together allowing the unit content and *Training* to inform your prayers.

LISTENING WORSHIP PLAYLIST
FOR PRAYER BOOT CAMP

Listening Worship Playlist on iTunes – Because Listening Worship is such an integral part of *Prayer Boot Camp*, we have made available on iTunes a Playlist for your use. You may access the Playlist in either of these ways:

- Go to www.hiddenmannaministry.com. Click on **Prayer Boot Camp**. Click on **Worship**. Click on **Prayer Boot Camp iMix**.
- Go to www.apple.com/iTunes. Enter "Prayer Boot Camp" in Search Store. Playlists will appear on the left side of the page. Click on **Prayer Boot Camp** playlist.

You may purchase the entire Playlist or individual songs directly from iTunes.

Unit 1 Worship, Stillness, Scripture

1. *See the Way* – Misty Edwards
2. *Soul Cry* – Misty Edwards

Unit 2 Invitation to Relationship

1. *Soul Cry* – Misty Edwards
2. *Where I Belong* – Cory Asbury

Unit 3 Confession and Repentance

1. *Where I Belong* – Cory Asbury
2. *You Will Not Relent* – David Brymer

Unit 4 Praying From the Inside Out

1. *You Will Not Relent* – David Brymer
2. *Beckon Me* – Mandy Rushing

Unit 5 Prayer of Rest

1. *Beckon Me* – Mandy Rushing
2. *You Made a Way* – Matt Gillman
3. *Carving Out A Place* – Laura Hackett

Unit 6 Recognizing The Voice of God

1. *You Made a Way* – Matt Gilman
2. *I Am Yours* – Misty Edwards

Unit 7 Stones of Remembrance

1. *I Am Yours* – Misty Edwards
2. *Jesus Let Me See Your Eyes* – Cory Asbury

Unit 8 Praying Like the Bride, Not the Widow

1. *Jesus Let Me See Your Eyes* – Cory Asbury
2. *Favorite One* – Misty Edwards

Unit 9 At The King's Table

1. *Favorite One* – Misty Edwards
2. *You Satisfy* – Julie Meyer

Unit 10 The Battle Ready Warrior

1. *You Satisfy* – Julie Meyer
2. *I Put On Christ* – Laura Hackett

Unit 11 The Overcoming Warrior

1. *I Put On Christ* – Laura Hackett
2. *Conquering Lion* – Grace Falkner

Unit 12 Beholding God

1. *Holy* – Matt Gilman
2. *My Beloved* – Cory Asbury

unit1 WORSHIP, STILLNESS AND SCRIPTURE

Open with a short prayer welcoming the presence of God and inviting group members to focus their attention on Him.

Allow 5 - 10 minutes for "listening worship" to quiet hearts and minds.

Close worship with a short prayer asking God for revelation as you begin the unit.

Read unit Introduction to the group slowly and clearly, allowing group members to listen and hear.

Worship Suggestions

* *See the Way* – Misty Edwards
* *Soul Cry* – Misty Edwards

Worship, Stillness and Scripture

Three streams run through the *Prayer Boot Camp* curriculum—**Centrality of Worship**, **Necessity of Stillness** and **Foundation of Scripture**. These streams of refreshing, renewal and revelation help move us into a place of deeper communion with the Father, the Son and the Holy Spirit.

How do worship, stillness and Scripture provide strategic advantage in the battle of your life? They prove to be key strategies to the sustainable victory in the battle for your identity, intimacy and authority in Christ.

We will return to these streams repeatedly as we explore core practices that enable us to cultivate the kind of prayer life Jesus modeled in His relationship with the Father. These practices invite us to live from a posture of celebration— resting in God's presence and trusting in His love—as we open our hearts to a greater revelation of His heart through the "daily bread" of Scripture.

Ask someone to read the Strategy. Continue around the circle taking turns slowly reading aloud and sharing together during the Reflection Questions.

Strategy

- **Worship is the foundation of all prayer.**
- **Stillness is the place we meet with God.**
- **Scripture is God's revealed heart to us.**

Centrality of Worship

- Worship and thanksgiving are the foundation of all prayer. Our God is a holy God and He alone is worthy of our praise.

  "Each of the four living creatures had six wings and was covered with eyes all around, even under his wings. Day and night they never stop saying: 'Holy, holy, holy is the Lord God Almighty, who was, and is, and is to come.' Whenever the living creatures give glory, honor and thanks to him who sits on the throne and who lives for ever and ever, the twenty-four elders fall down before him who sits on the throne, and worship him who lives for ever and ever. They lay their crowns before the throne and say: 'You are worthy, our Lord and God, to receive glory and honor and power, for you created all things, and by your will they were created and have their being.'" (Revelation 4:8-11)

- Worship takes the focus away from us and puts it on God.

  "Come, let us bow down in worship, let us kneel before the LORD our Maker; for he is our God and we are the people of his pasture, the flock under his care." (Psalm 95:6-7)

- We invite the presence of God when we worship Him.

  "Let us go to his dwelling place; let us worship at his footstool – arise, O LORD, and come to your resting place, you and the ark of your might." (Psalm 132:7-8)

- Join the heavenly chorus in worship by together reading aloud these words from Revelation 4:

  (ALL) "Holy, holy, holy is the Lord God Almighty, who was, and is, and is to come.... You are worthy, our Lord and God, to receive glory and honor and power, for you created all things, and by your will they were created and have their being." (Revelation 4:8; 11)

Reflection Question:

Have you ever considered reading Scripture aloud as a form of worship? What are some ways you worship God?

_____

_____

Read the Reflection Question and allow each person a few moments to respond.

Necessity of Stillness

◆ We come to know God as we take time to be still.

"Be still, and know that I am God." (Psalm 46:10)

◆ Stillness requires us to quiet our thoughts and actions. God reveals His ways, His heart and His character when we are still in His presence.

"My soul finds rest in God alone; my salvation comes from him." (Psalm 62:1)

◆ Stillness shifts us into a listening position. At the Transfiguration, the Father gave only one command to Jesus' followers:

"This is my Son, whom I love; with him I am well pleased. Listen to him." (Matthew 17:5)

◆ We tend to pray out of our own empathies, sympathies and wishes. God desires that we learn to pray out of the promptings of His Spirit, carefully listening as we pray.

"But when he, the Spirit of truth, comes, he will guide you into all truth. He will not speak on his own; he will speak only what he hears, and he will tell you what is yet to come. He will bring glory to me by taking from what is mine and making it known to you." (John 16:13-14)

Reflection Question:

Does the idea of 'stillness' present a challenge or invitation for you in prayer?

_____

_____

Read the Reflection Question and allow each person a few moments to respond.

Worship, Stillness and Scripture are key to victory in the battle for your identity, intimacy and authority in Christ.

Foundation of Scripture

"Your word, O LORD, is eternal; it stands firm in the heavens." (Psalm 119:89)

◆ God's Word is alive. By His Word He spoke the world into existence.

"For the word of God is living and active. Sharper than any double-edged sword, it penetrates even to dividing soul and spirit, joints and marrow; it judges the thoughts and attitudes of the heart. Nothing in all creation is hidden from God's sight. Everything is uncovered and laid bare before the eyes of him to whom we must give account." (Hebrews 4:12-13)

◆ Praying God's Word is powerful. It releases His light and illuminates our understanding.

"The unfolding of your words gives light; it gives understanding to the simple." (Psalm 119:130)

◆ There is nothing we can say more rightly in prayer than what has already been set forth in Scripture.

"All Scripture is God-breathed and is useful for teaching, rebuking, correcting and training in righteousness, so that the man of God may be thoroughly equipped for every good work." (2 Timothy 3:16-17)

Reflection Question:

How has Scripture shaped your prayers or prayer experience?

_____

_____

Read the Reflection Question and allow each person a few moments to respond.

Ask someone to read the Strategy Recap.

Strategy Recap

- **Worship is the foundation of all prayer.**
- **Stillness is the place we meet with God.**
- **Scripture is God's revealed heart to us.**

Training

Read through the Training silently. Read through it again, this time stopping to rest in the Word and respond to what God reveals. (20 Minutes)

Read Psalm 46:

"God is our refuge and strength, an ever-present help in trouble. Therefore we will not fear, though the earth give way and the mountains fall into the heart of the sea, though its waters roar and foam and the mountains quake with their surging. Selah. There is a river whose streams make glad the city of God, the holy place where the Most High dwells. God is within her, she will not fall; God will help her at break of day. Nations are in uproar, kingdoms fall; he lifts his voice, the earth melts. The LORD Almighty is with us; the God of Jacob is our fortress. Selah. Come and see the works of the LORD, the desolations he has brought on the earth. He makes wars cease to the ends of the earth; he breaks the bow and shatters the spear, he burns the shields with fire. Be still, and know that I am God; I will be exalted among the nations, I will be exalted in the earth. The LORD Almighty is with us; the God of Jacob is our fortress. Selah."

Rest

- Focus on coming before the throne of God.

- Invite the Holy Spirit to be present and to help you hear the Father.

- Bring your mind and heart to rest as you come before Him in alert stillness.

- Release all distractions as you surrender to His presence.

- Refocus on the words of Psalm 46 if your mind wanders.

- Receive God's invitation to be still and know that He is God.

Respond

- Record what God has revealed. How does this psalm speak to you regarding:

  Worship

  Stillness

  Scripture

- Rejoice in who God is.

Share

- Share with your group what God is showing you.

Pray

- Worship together with verbal praises to God using Psalm 46 to inform your prayers.
  Example: *"We praise you because you are our refuge and strength."*

The practice of alert stillness helps us hear from God.

Going Deeper exercises are designed for use in personal quiet time with God between sessions.

Facilitator:
Close with a short prayer or the Lord's Prayer. If time permits you may pray together allowing the unit content and Training to inform your prayers. At the end of Closing Prayer, ask for a volunteer to facilitate the group at the next meeting.

Going Deeper

Choose psalms from the following list and repeat the Training exercise on the previous page:

- Psalm 42
- Psalm 84
- Psalm 103
- Psalm 121
- Psalm 130

unit 2 INVITATION TO RELATIONSHIP

Open with a short prayer welcoming the presence of God and inviting group members to focus their attention on Him.

Allow 5 - 10 minutes for "listening worship" to quiet hearts and minds.

Close worship with a short prayer asking God for revelation as you begin the unit.

Read unit Introduction to the group slowly and clearly, allowing group members to listen and hear.

Worship Suggestions

- *Soul Cry* – Misty Edwards
- *Where I Belong* – Cory Asbury

Invitation to Relationship

God is not particularly interested in religion. What He really cares about is relationship.

The world tends to distort the true identity of God. We may end up worshiping idols and broken images rather than worshiping "in spirit and in truth." In the same way, the world holds up broken mirrors to who we are in Christ. When we believe what the world says about us, we are weakened in our ability to walk with God as His Beloved and to contend for the victory we have in Christ.

As John the Baptist said, "He must become greater. I must become less." Therein lies the key to our transformation in relationship to Jesus. When our understanding of who *we* are begins to line up with the reality of who *God* is, then we begin to experience spiritual authority and victory in the battle for our life.

Ask someone to read the Strategy. Continue around the circle taking turns slowly reading aloud and sharing together during the Reflection Questions.

 ## Strategy

Knowing through Scripture who God is, and who we are in Him:

- ◆ **Establishes His authority.**
- ◆ **Reveals our true identity.**
- ◆ **Builds right relationship.**

Centrality of Worship

We experience victory when our understanding of who we are begins to line up with the reality of who God is.

◆ Worshiping God establishes the context for our relationship with Him. It brings us to a place of surrender where we can yield our will to His. When we worship in spirit and in truth, God has a way of exposing our perspectives and agendas and revealing His.

"For this is what the high and lofty One says—he who lives forever, whose name is holy: 'I live in a high and holy place, but also with him who is contrite and lowly in spirit, to revive the spirit of the lowly and to revive the heart of the contrite.'" (Isaiah 57:15)

◆ Worship aligns our perspective with God's power and dominion. The little things that used to matter so much become unimportant as He gives us eyes to see the bigger picture of what is happening around us.

"When I tried to understand all this, it was oppressive to me till I entered the sanctuary of God." (Psalm 73:16-17)

Reflection Question:

Read the Reflection Question and allow each person a few moments to respond.

What stands out for you in these ideas about worship? Why?

_____

_____

Necessity of Stillness

◆ Getting to know someone is always the first step in any relationship. We never get to know another person if we do all the talking!

"Know that the LORD is God. It is he who made us, and we are his; we are his people, the sheep of his pasture." (Psalm 100:3)

- Stillness is the place we meet alone with God.

  "Then, because so many people were coming and going that they did not even have a chance to eat, he said to them, 'Come with me by yourselves to a quiet place and get some rest.'" (Mark 6:31)

- Waiting and listening in stillness sets the order of right relationship to God. He becomes greater while we become less.

  "The bride belongs to the bridegroom. The friend who attends the bridegroom waits and listens for him, and is full of joy when he hears the bridegroom's voice. That joy is mine, and it is now complete. He must become greater; I must become less." (John 3:29-30)

Reflection Question:

What do you think about the role of stillness in your relationship with God?

_____

_____

Foundation of Scripture

- Scripture helps us to accurately know God. It expands our knowledge of Him and reveals what He desires for us.

  "Come to me, all you who are weary and burdened, and I will give you rest. Take my yoke upon you and learn from me, for I am gentle and humble in heart, and you will find rest for your souls. For my yoke is easy and my burden is light." (Matthew 11:28-30)

- Scripture enables us to have relationship with God that is based on facts, not feelings. A relationship based on feelings, rather than truth, leaves us wide-open for disappointment, anger and resentment if God doesn't respond the way we expect.

  "God said to Moses, 'I am who I am.'" (Exodus 3:14)

  "God is not a man, that he should lie, nor a son of man, that he should change his mind. Does he speak and then not act? Does he promise and not fulfill?" (Numbers 23:19)

- Scripture helps us see ourselves through God's eyes. Without it, we have an inaccurate view of who He is and who we are in Christ.

Without Scripture, we have an inaccurate view of who God is and who we are in Christ.

Read the Reflection Question and allow each person a few moments to respond.

The world holds up broken mirrors to who we are in Christ.

"But you are a chosen people, a royal priesthood, a holy nation, a people belonging to God, that you may declare the praises of him who called you out of darkness into his wonderful light." (1 Peter 2:9)

"Let the beloved of the LORD rest secure in him, for he shields him all day long, and the one the LORD loves rests between his shoulders." (Deuteronomy 33:12)

◆ It's important to know how God sees us so we can consciously come out of agreement with the lies of the enemy and into agreement with God.

"Behold, You desire truth in the inward parts, and in the hidden part You will make me to know wisdom." (Psalm 51:6 NKJV)

Reflection Question:

Does your relationship with God tend to rely on facts or feelings?

Read the Reflection Question and allow each person a few moments to respond.

Ask someone to read the Strategy Recap.

Strategy Recap

Knowing through Scripture who God is, and who we are in Him:

- ◆ **Establishes His authority.**
- ◆ **Reveals our true identity.**
- ◆ **Builds right relationship.**

Training
Names of God

Group Exercise

Take turns reading aloud through Names of God, each person speaking one name, pausing in between.
Personalize them. Example: "You are my Abba Father."
(Scripture citations are for reference only. They do not need to be read aloud.)

You are:

Abba Father – (Romans 8:15)
Author & Perfecter of Faith – (Hebrews 12:2)
Bridegroom – (John 3:29)
Burden Bearer – (Psalm 55:22 NKJV)
Compassionate – (Matthew 9:36)
Counselor – (John 14:16-17)
Dwelling Place – (Psalm 90:1)
Defender & Defense – (Jeremiah 50:34)
Ever Present Help – (Psalm 46:1)
Enthroned – (Isaiah 40:22)
Faithful & True – (Revelation 19:11)
Friend – (John 15:13)
Generous – (1 Timothy 6:17)
Gentle & Humble – (Matthew 11:29)
Hiding Place – (Psalm 32:7)
Healer – (Psalm 147:3)
Immanuel (God with us) – (Matthew 1:23)
Intercessor – (Hebrews 7:25)
Jehovah Jireh (Our Provider) – (Genesis 22:14)
Jealous – (2 Corinthians 11:2)
King of Glory – (Psalm 24:7)
Keeper – (Psalm 121:5-7)
Living Water – (Revelation 7:17)

Merciful – (Numbers 14:18)
Mediator – (1 Timothy 2:5)
Near – (Psalm 145:18)
Never Failing – (Joshua 23:14)
Offering for Sin – (Romans 8:3)
Overcomer – (Revelation 17:14)
Peace – (Ephesians 2:14)
Portion – (Psalm 73:26)
Quieter of the Storm – (Psalm 107:29)
Refuge – (Psalm 91:2)
Restorer of my Soul – (Psalm 23:3)
Shield – (Psalm 3:3)
Sanctuary – (Isaiah 8:13-14)
Trustworthy – (Psalm 111:7)
Truth – (John 14:6)
Unchanging – (Malachi 3:6)
Understanding – (Psalm 147:5)
Vindicator – (Jeremiah 51:10)
Wonderful – (Isaiah 9:6)
Worthy – (Revelation 4:11)
Yesterday & Forever the Same – (Hebrews 13:8)
Zealous – (Isaiah 9:7)

Alone with God

Facilitator – Allow 5 minutes of silence to consider the following before moving on to the next page.

• After reading through *Names of God* with your group, are there any names that do not align with what you believe to be true of Him?

• Ask Him to let this name become real to you.

Training
My Identity in Christ

Group Exercise

Take turns reading aloud through My Identity in Christ, each person speaking one attribute, pausing in between. Make it your own. Example: "I am able to do all things."
(Scripture citations are for reference only. They do not need to be read aloud.)

I am:

Able to do all things – (Philippians 4:13)
Accepted – (Romans 15:7)
Adequate – (2 Corinthians 3:5 NASB)
Beautiful – (Song of Songs 1:15)
Beloved – (Deuteronomy 33:12)
Bride – (Revelation 21:9)
Bold & Confident – (Ephesians 3:12 NKJV)
Chosen – (Colossians 3:12; I Peter 1:2)
Dead to sin, alive to God – (Romans 6:11)
Delivered – (2 Corinthians 1:9-10)
Encouraged – (2 Thessalonians 2:16-17)
Equipped – (2 Timothy 3:17)
Favored – (Psalm 84:11)
Friend of God – (John 15:14-15)
Hidden with Christ in God – (Colossians 3:3)
Holy – (Hebrews 10:10)
Inscribed on His palms – (Isaiah 49:16 NKJV)
Inseparable from His love – (Romans 8:35)
Joint heir with Christ – (Romans 8:17 NKJV)
Justified – (1 Corinthians 6:11)
Known – (Psalm 139:1)
Light of the world – (Matthew 5:14)

Made by Him – (Psalm 100:3)
New creation – (2 Corinthians 5:17)
Never forsaken – (Hebrews 13:5)
One with Him – (John 17:23 NKJV)
Overcomer – (1 John 5:4-5)
Perfect & complete – (James 1:2-4 NKJV)
Prayed for – (Romans 8:27)
Qualified to share His inheritance – (Colossians 1:12)
Redeemed – (Galatians 3:13)
Renewed – (2 Corinthians 4:16)
Salt of the earth – (Matthew 5:13)
Soldier – (2 Timothy 2:3-4)
Spiritually minded – (Romans 8:6)
Temple of the Holy Spirit – (1 Corinthians 6:19)
Treasured – (Psalm 83:3 NASB)
Under no condemnation – (Romans 8:1)
United with Christ – (Romans 6:5)
Valued – (Matthew 6:26)
Victorious – (1 Corinthians 15:57)
Washed, sanctified, justified – (1 Corinthians 6:11)
His witness – (Acts 1:8)
Yielded to God – (Romans 6:13)

Alone with God

Facilitator – Allow 5 minutes of silence to consider the following before moving on to the next page.

♦ After reading through *My Identity in Christ* with your group, are there any aspects of your identity in Him that do not align with what you believe to be true of yourself?

♦ Ask God to let His Word settle as truth in your heart.

Training Group Exercise

Group Exercise *(Facilitator leads)*

SHARE:

- ◆ What name of God means the most to you and why?
- ◆ Are there names of God that you struggle with? Explain.
- ◆ What identity in Christ means the most to you and why?
- ◆ Are there identities in Christ that you struggle with? Explain.

If time permits, use the previous pages to declare aloud in prayer the Names of God and your Identity in Christ.

Facilitator:
Close with a short prayer or the Lord's Prayer. If time permits you may pray together allowing the unit content and Training to inform your prayers. At the end of Closing Prayer, ask for a volunteer to facilitate the group at the next meeting.

Going Deeper

Going Deeper exercises are designed for use in personal quiet time with God between sessions.

During periods of stress or sleeplessness, declare names of God and who you are in Christ as you work through the alphabet by letter. Rest in them.

unit 3 CONFESSION AND REPENTANCE

Open with a short prayer welcoming the presence of God and inviting group members to focus their attention on Him.

Allow 5 - 10 minutes for "listening worship" to quiet hearts and minds.

Close worship with a short prayer asking God for revelation as you begin the unit.

Read unit Introduction to the group slowly and clearly, allowing group members to listen and hear.

Worship Suggestions

◆ *Where I Belong* – Cory Asbury
◆ *You Will Not Relent* – David Brymer

Confession and Repentance

The power of repentance in a believer's life is enormous. It would be hard to overstate its role in the ongoing redemption, purification and empowering of God's people. Our resistance to experiencing true confession and repentance keeps us from abundant life in Christ.

Repentance is a gift. It liberates us from sin and bondage to decay so that we may be transformed into the likeness of Christ. But we cannot experience true repentance until we have understood the nature of sin in our lives—that which we recognize so readily in others yet so often fail to see in ourselves.

What is sin? Anything less than the glory of God. Anything short of His holiness. Any failure to conform to the moral law of God in act, attitude or nature is sin. Seen in the light of God's unblemished radiance, we begin to grapple with the corruption inherent in our sinful nature. For the heart of man is deceitful above all else. But the grace of God through the blood of Christ is sufficient to wash us whiter than snow and enable us to come before the throne of grace with confidence.

Ask someone to read the Strategy. Continue around the circle taking turns slowly reading aloud and sharing together during the Reflection Questions.

Strategy

Know and embrace the power of:

- **Confession – Admission of sin and its consequences.**
- **Repentance – Forsaking sin and turning to God.**
- **Restoration – Freedom to walk in right relationship with God.**

Centrality of Worship

◆ Genuine encounter with God in worship causes us to be undone. When we experience the holiness of God, we are able to comprehend the gap between His holiness and our sinfulness.

"And they were calling to one another: 'Holy, holy, holy is the LORD Almighty; the whole earth is full of his glory.' At the sound of their voices the doorposts and thresholds shook and the temple was filled with smoke. 'Woe to me!' I cried. 'I am ruined! For I am a man of unclean lips, and I live among a people of unclean lips, and my eyes have seen the King, the LORD Almighty.'" (Isaiah 6:3-5)

◆ Worship brings us into agreement with the holiness of God and compels us to examine our hearts before Him.

"Search me, O God, and know my heart; test me and know my anxious thoughts. See if there is any offensive way in me, and lead me in the way everlasting." (Psalm 139:23-24)

◆ We tend to avoid honest confrontation with personal sin. Yet, confession and repentance are God's way of cleansing us in the righteous blood of Jesus, freeing us to worship Him in spirit and in truth.

"Repent, then, and turn to God, so that your sins may be wiped out, that times of refreshing may come from the Lord." (Acts 3:19)

◆ True repentance is a profound expression of worship.

"In the same way, I tell you, there is rejoicing in the presence of the angels of God over one sinner who repents." (Luke 15:10)

Reflection Question:

Have you ever thought of repentance as worship? How might lack of confession and repentance compromise your worship?

Read the Reflection Question and allow each person a few moments to respond.

_____

_____

Necessity of Stillness

True repentance is a profound expression of worship.

◆ Stillness helps us hear the Lord speak truth in the secret places of our hearts. Repentance comes when we allow the Holy Spirit to search our inward being.

"Surely you desire truth in the inner parts. You teach me wisdom in the inmost place." (Psalm 51:6)

"In repentance and rest is your salvation, in quietness and trust is your strength, but you would have none of it. Yet the Lord longs to be gracious to you; he rises to show you compassion. For the Lord is a God of Justice. Blessed are all who wait for him!" (Isaiah 30:15,18)

◆ A contrite heart does not attempt to rationalize, excuse or defend sin. It draws near in confession, quietly trusting in God's forgiveness.

"If we claim to be without sin, we deceive ourselves and the truth is not in us. If we confess our sins, he is faithful and just and will forgive us our sins and purify us from all unrighteousness." (1 John 1:8-9)

"Rend your heart and not your garments. Return to the LORD your God, for he is gracious and compassionate, slow to anger and abounding in love, and he relents from sending calamity." (Joel 2:13)

◆ Repentance is a gift. It draws us nearer to God and opens the door for our transformation.

"Rid yourselves of all the offenses you have committed and get a new heart and a new spirit." (Ezekiel 18:31)

"God exalted him to his own right hand as Prince and Savior that he might *give* repentance and forgiveness of sins to Israel." (Acts 5:31 *Emphasis added*)

◆ The Posture of Repentance: Prayer brings us to our knees before God. Repentance puts us on our faces.

"Godly sorrow brings repentance that leads to salvation and leaves no regret, but worldly sorrow brings death." (2 Corinthians 7:10)

"The LORD is good to those whose hope is in him, to the one who seeks him. . . . Let him sit alone in silence, for the LORD has laid it on him. Let him bury his face in the dust—there may yet be hope." (Lamentations 3:25, 28-29)

Reflection Question:

How have you experienced the 'gift' of repentance in your journey with Jesus?

Read the Reflection Question and allow each person a few moments to respond.

Sin disrupts God's design for intimacy.

Foundation of Scripture

◆ God's Word is a searchlight on our souls. Godly sorrow that wells up in response to Scripture is the Holy Spirit's way of bringing us to repentance.

"For the word of God is living and active. Sharper than any double-edged sword, it penetrates even to dividing soul and spirit, joints and marrow; it judges the thoughts and attitudes of the heart. Nothing in all creation is hidden from God's sight. Everything is uncovered and laid bare before the eyes of him to whom we must give account." (Hebrews 4:12-13)

◆ Conviction from the Holy Spirit brings us to repentance which sets us free, drawing us closer to God.

"When he [the Holy Spirit] comes, he will convict the world of guilt in regard to sin and righteousness and judgment . . ." (John 16:8)

"There is now no condemnation for those who are in Christ Jesus because through Christ Jesus the law of the Spirit of life set me free from the law of sin and death." (Romans 8:1-2)

◆ Condemnation is the enemy's ploy to keep us in bondage to guilt and shame which separates us from God. We are no longer subject to condemnation because the blood of Jesus has set us free.

"Be self-controlled and alert. Your enemy the devil prowls around like a roaring lion looking for someone to devour." (1 Peter 5:8)

"Then I heard a loud voice in heaven say: 'Now have come the salvation and the power and the kingdom of our God, and the authority of his Christ. For the accuser of our brothers, who accuses them before our God day and night, has been hurled down.'" (Revelation 12:10)

◆ When God illuminates the broken and bound up places in your life, quickly confess and repent before the Lord. This is the path to freedom.

"Then I acknowledged my sin to you and did not cover up my iniquity. I said, 'I will confess my transgressions to the LORD'— and you forgave the guilt of my sin. Selah." (Psalm 32:5)

◆ Just as God has poured out forgiveness on our sin, so must we be diligent to forgive those who wound us. Unforgiveness keeps us in bondage to sin.

"For if you forgive men when they sin against you, your heavenly Father will also forgive you. But if you do not forgive men their sins, your Father will not forgive your sins." (Matthew 6:14-15)

◆ God's original desire is that we walk with Him. Sin disrupts His design for intimacy. God's Word is meant to wash away the residue of living in a sinful world. Spend time daily in His Word.

"'Come now, let us reason together,' says the LORD. 'Though your sins are like scarlet, they shall be as white as snow; though they are red as crimson, they shall be like wool. If you are willing and obedient, you will eat the best from the land; but if you resist and rebel, you will be devoured by the sword.' For the mouth of the LORD has spoken." (Isaiah 1:18-20)

Reflection Question:

Are you able to discern the difference between conviction and condemnation? Ask God to help you distinguish between godly conviction and unholy condemnation.

_____

_____

For Clarity

Sin	**Anything less than the glory of God.**
Conviction	**A piercing sense of our sinfulness.**
Confession	**Humble admission of our sin and its consequence.**
Repentance	**Heartfelt grief and forsaking of sin so that we may return to God.**
Forgiveness	**Receiving God's absolute release from all condemnation for sin.**
Restoration	**Freedom to walk in unencumbered relationship with God.**

Condemnation is the enemy's ploy to keep us in bondage to guilt and shame.

Read the Reflection Question and allow each person a few moments to respond.

Ask someone to read For Clarity.

Ask someone to read the Strategy Recap.

Strategy Recap

Confession and Repentance:

- Break agreement with sin and strongholds, leading to freedom.
- Bring redemption, restoration and blessing, evoking gratitude for God's mercy.
- Help us discern conviction, the pathway to confession and repentance.
- Help us discern that condemnation is a dead end leading to bondage.

Training

Facilitator: Read Training instructions aloud to the group. Ask if there are questions. Allow 15 - 20 minutes for group members to silently read and consider the list below. After silent time, invite the group to share what the Lord has revealed.

"If I had cherished sin in my heart, the Lord would not have listened." (Psalm 66:18)

READ this list of prompts. As you pause with each word, ask the Holy Spirit to reveal any 'little foxes' of sin that have crept into your vineyard—(Song of Solomon 2:15). Feel free to add to the list as the Lord leads.

Anger	Jealousy	Selfishness
Resentment	Offense	Anxiety
Unforgiveness	Pride	Doubt
Hurt	Exaggeration	Despair
Bitterness	Gossip	Avarice
Retaliation	Complaint	Lust
Impatience	Cold heart	Discourtesy
Critical Spirit	Idolatry	Indulgence
Judgmental Spirit	Laziness	Control
Superiority	Self-Pity	Manipulation
Envy	Phoniness	Perfectionism

- ◆ **CONFESS** any area of sin that stirs conviction in your heart. Bring these before God.
- ◆ **REPENT** of any sin which grieves your spirit. Pray.
- ◆ **RESOLVE** with the help of the Holy Spirit to turn away from sin and return to God in this matter.
- ◆ **RECEIVE** His love and forgiveness with a grateful heart. You are His Beloved!

The path to freedom through confession and repentance is an ongoing journey.

Invite the Lord to show you areas of sin where He wants to set you free.

"Therefore confess your sins to each other and pray for each other so that you may be healed."
(James 5:16)

SHARE with your group what the Lord is revealing to you.

**Repentance
is a gift.**

Going Deeper exercises are designed for use in personal quiet time with God between sessions.

Going Deeper

Meditate on Psalm 51.

- Allow your heart to be moved by the burden of your sin.
- When you are ready, write a psalm that expresses your grief and gratitude, distress and desire for cleansing.
- Pray your psalm aloud to Him.
- Acknowledge His mercy and forgiveness. Let your praise arise.

Deeper Still

- Ask the Lord about a period of fasting in pursuit of repentance.

unit 4 PRAYING FROM THE INSIDE OUT

Worship Suggestions

- *You Will Not Relent* – David Brymer
- *Beckon Me* – Mandy Rushing

Praying From The Inside Out

By allowing the Holy Spirit to purify our hearts through the ongoing process of confession, repentance and restoration, we are liberated to pray according to the plumb line of Christ in our inmost being.

Man looks at the outside. God sees the heart. For this reason, Jesus rejected external forms and rituals that had no bearing on the inner reality and condition of the heart. When He found the temple defiled by money changers and marketplace substitutes for authentic worship, He turned the tables upside down, driving out every vestige of false religion in order to restore the temple to its rightful purpose. "It is written, 'My house shall be called a house of prayer; but you have made it a den of thieves.'" (Matthew 21:13 NKJV)

Today, we are His temple. When our hearts are drawn into alignment with Christ, we are able to pray with authority according to His heart rather than our own good ideas. "Unless the Lord builds the house, its builders labor in vain. Unless the Lord watches over the city, the watchmen stand guard in vain." (Psalm 127:1) As we allow the Lord to put our spiritual house in order, we can then step into ever-widening arenas of spiritual influence as watchmen on His wall. This is the essence of praying from the inside out.

Ask someone to read the Strategy. Continue around the circle taking turns slowly reading aloud and sharing together during the Reflection Questions.

Spirit inspired prayer flows from right alignment with God's heart.

Strategy

- **Recognize your God-given circle of influence and authority in prayer.**
- **Embrace the personal prayer assignments God has for you.**
- **Release the burden of carrying other people's prayer expectations.**
- **Enlarge your circles of intercession from the inside out.**

Centrality of Worship

- Seeking God in worship brings us into His throne room. Standing in His courts, we hear His heart for us and for the circumstances and people He places around us.

  "One thing I ask of the LORD, this is what I seek: that I may dwell in the house of the LORD all the days of my life, to gaze upon the beauty of the LORD and to seek him in his temple." (Psalm 27:4)

- Being in God's presence changes us, reshaping our will and emotions. Out of His presence, we are best able to express the heart of God.

  "But whenever anyone turns to the Lord, the veil is taken away. Now the Lord is the Spirit, and where the Spirit of the Lord is, there is freedom. And we, who with unveiled faces all reflect the Lord's glory, are being transformed into his likeness with ever-increasing glory, which comes from the Lord, who is the Spirit." (2 Corinthians 3:16-18)

- Spirit-inspired prayer flows from right alignment with God's heart. This is the starting place for praying from the inside out.

  "Therefore, I urge you, brothers, in view of God's mercy, to offer your bodies as living sacrifices, holy and pleasing to God—this is your spiritual act of worship. Do not conform any longer to the pattern of this world, but be transformed by the renewing of your mind. Then you will be able to test and approve what God's will is—his good, pleasing and perfect will." (Romans 12:1-2)

- A lifestyle of worship brings us into intimacy with God, filling us with Him. Our prayers then express the goodness of God for those people and circumstances He brings to our attention.

  "The good man brings good things out of the good stored up in his heart, and the evil man brings evil things out of the evil stored up in his heart. For out of the overflow of his heart his mouth speaks." (Luke 6:45)

- We best serve others in prayer when our inmost being is satisfied with God.

"My soul will be satisfied as with the richest of foods; with singing lips my mouth will praise you." (Psalm 63:5)

Reflection Question:

How might worship be a starting place for an effective prayer life?
What are some worldly patterns that keep you from intimate worship?

Read the Reflection Question and allow each person a few moments to respond.

Necessity of Stillness

◆ Stillness opens the door for the Holy Spirit to stir and direct our prayers for the people, places and circumstances in our lives.

"In the same way, the Spirit helps us in our weakness. We do not know what we ought to pray for, but the Spirit himself intercedes for us with groans that words cannot express." (Romans 8:26)

◆ Humble yourselves before the Father, asking Him to stir your heart with the burdens of His heart. Confidently expect Him to meet complex needs through simple prayers.

"LORD, my heart is not haughty, nor my eyes lofty. Neither do I concern myself with great matters, nor with things too profound for me." (Psalm 131:1 NKJV)

◆ Inner stillness is a journey that brings us to the point of absolute trust in the Lord.

"Surely I have calmed and quieted my soul, like a weaned child with his mother; like a weaned child is my soul within me." (Psalm 131:2 NKJV)

◆ Rest in the knowledge that your heavenly Father already knows your needs and is more than able to provide for them out of the abundance of His heart.

"But seek first his kingdom and his righteousness, and all these things will be given to you as well." (Matthew 6:33)

Who you are at home is who you are in God's Kingdom.

Reflection Question:

Do you confidently expect God to meet complex needs through your simple prayers?
Or do you feel compelled to explain your needs and desired results?

Read the Reflection Question and allow each person a few moments to respond.

Let your present
reality inform your
prayer priority.

Foundation of Scripture

◆ Focus first on keeping your spiritual house in order. Who you are at home is who you are in God's Kingdom.

"Therefore, if you are offering your gift at the altar and there remember that your brother has something against you, leave your gift there in front of the altar. First go and be reconciled to your brother; then come and offer your gift." (Matthew 5:23-24)

◆ Praying for the people and circumstances closest to us is training for praying effectively for the larger world around us. Our authority in the kingdom is only as strong as the weakest part of our lives.

"If anyone says, 'I love God,' yet hates his brother, he is a liar. For anyone who does not love his brother, whom he has seen, cannot love God, whom he has not seen." (1 John 4:20)

◆ Caution. Your unfinished personal business with God will hinder your ability to pray according to the Father's Word and will for the Kingdom.

"First clean the inside of the cup and dish, and then the outside also will be clean." (Matthew 23:26)

◆ His Word provides the foundation and authority for praying in agreement with the will of God. Let the Lord give you His heart so that you will know how to pray for each situation.

"If you remain in me and my words remain in you, ask whatever you wish, and it will be given you. This is to my Father's glory, that you bear much fruit, showing yourselves to be my disciples." (John 15:7-8)

◆ Notice recurring patterns and circumstances which may be subtle invitations from God. Respond by inquiring of Him. He may be using them to give you a prayer assignment.

"Then the LORD called Samuel. Samuel answered, 'Here I am.' And he ran to Eli and said, 'Here I am; you called me.' But Eli said, 'I did not call; go back and lie down.' So he went and lay down. Again the LORD called, 'Samuel!' And Samuel got up and went to Eli and said, 'Here I am; you called me.' 'My son,' Eli said, 'I did not call; go back and lie down. . . .' The LORD called Samuel a third time, and Samuel got up and went to Eli and said, 'Here I am; you called me.' Then Eli realized that the LORD was calling the boy. So Eli told Samuel, 'Go and lie down, and if he calls you, say, "Speak, LORD, for your servant is listening."'" (1 Samuel 3:4-6, 8-9)

- Let your present reality inform your prayer priority. God is trusting you in that place.

  "For if you remain completely silent at this time, relief and deliverance will arise for the Jews from another place, but you and your father's house will perish. Yet who knows whether you have come to the kingdom for such a time as this?" (Esther 4:14 NKJV)

- Freedom to take up our God-given prayer assignments releases us from the burden of carrying other people's prayer expectations.

  "Walk with me and work with me—watch how I do it. Learn the unforced rhythms of grace. I won't lay anything heavy or ill-fitting on you." (Matthew 11:29 The Message)

- Discern those assignments God is giving you. When you sense a prayer assignment from God, stand in that place until He releases you to stand in another place.

  "I will stand at my watch and station myself on the ramparts; I will look to see what he will say to me, and what answer I am to give to this complaint." (Habakkuk 2:1)

Reflection Question:

Do you see ways that unfinished personal business with God can be an obstacle to prayer? Has there been a time when God's Word challenged you to change the focus of your prayers or the way you were praying?

Read the Reflection Question and allow each person a few moments to respond.

_____

_____

For Clarity

Ask someone to read For Clarity.

Intercession	**Prayer on behalf of another.**
Prayer Request	**Praying a specific prayer at a specific time in loving response to a particular person's need.**
Prayer Assignment	**Carrying a burden or passion in prayer for a season as the Holy Spirit leads.**

Distinguishing between requests and assignments avoids misplaced prayer burdens.

Ask someone to read the Strategy Recap.

Strategy Recap

Inside out prayer:

- ◆ **Equips you to express the heart of God in prayer.**
- ◆ **Allows your present reality to inform your prayer priority.**
- ◆ **Helps you identify your personal prayer assignments.**
- ◆ **Releases you from the burden of carrying other people's prayer expectations.**

Training

Facilitator –Read the Training Exercise to the group. Allow 10 - 15 minutes of quiet time for group members to read through and consider the reflection below. At the end of this time, invite the group to share what God is showing them.

Identifying Prayer Assignments

God often uses people and circumstances around us to stir our hearts with the burdens of His heart. Sometimes He allows specific people or circumstances to repeatedly appear in our lives in order to reveal a prayer assignment.

Reflect on Habakkuk 2:1

> "I will climb up to my watchtower and stand at my guardpost. There I will wait to see what the Lord says and how he will answer my complaint." (Habakkuk 2:1 NLT)

Identify and list:

- Needs and concerns beyond your own that are frequently on your mind.
- Specific needs that others continually bring to you for prayer, resulting in a whole list of prayer requests on the same subject.
- Burdens of your heart, outside your own concerns, that repeatedly press you to prayer.
- Specific people who persistently surface in your mind.

Bring this list before God and ask Him to show you if these are indeed prayer assignments He may have for you. Our natural inclination is to respond emotionally when we are troubled or disturbed. What do you think a prayer response might look like in each of these situations? How would that differ from an emotional response?

Consider how the Lord may be speaking to you at this time. Is He calling you to any specific prayer assignment?

SHARE with your group what God is showing you.

Going Deeper exercises are designed for use in personal quiet time with God between sessions.

Facilitator:
Close with a short prayer or the Lord's Prayer. If time permits you may pray together allowing the unit content and Training to inform your prayers. At the end of Closing Prayer, ask for a volunteer to facilitate the group at the next meeting.

Going Deeper

"Unless the LORD builds the house, its builders labor in vain. Unless the LORD watches over the city, the watchmen stand guard in vain." (Psalm 127:1)

Praying from the inside out invites God to:

- ◆ Deal with whatever is in the deepest part of our own hearts first.
- ◆ Deal with whatever is right in front of us next.
- ◆ Teach us to pray for matters that make our hearts cry or sing as we learn to view the world through God's eyes.

"But you will receive power when the Holy Spirit comes on you; and you will be my witnesses in Jerusalem, and in all Judea and Samaria, and to the ends of the earth." (Acts 1:8)

After establishing intimate relationship with His disciples, Jesus invited them to be His witnesses, beginning with the most familiar places and moving outward through ever-widening spheres of influence.

- ◆ **Jerusalem** represents our center of most intimate life & worship.
- ◆ **Judea** represents the larger neighborhood and community in which we live.
- ◆ **Samaria** represents our less familiar regional neighbor alienated for their differing cultural identity.
- ◆ **Ends of the earth** represents our broadest spheres of Kingdom reach and influence.

Use the following illustration to help you identify your spheres of prayer influence. Remember that these spheres are both progressive and concurrent.

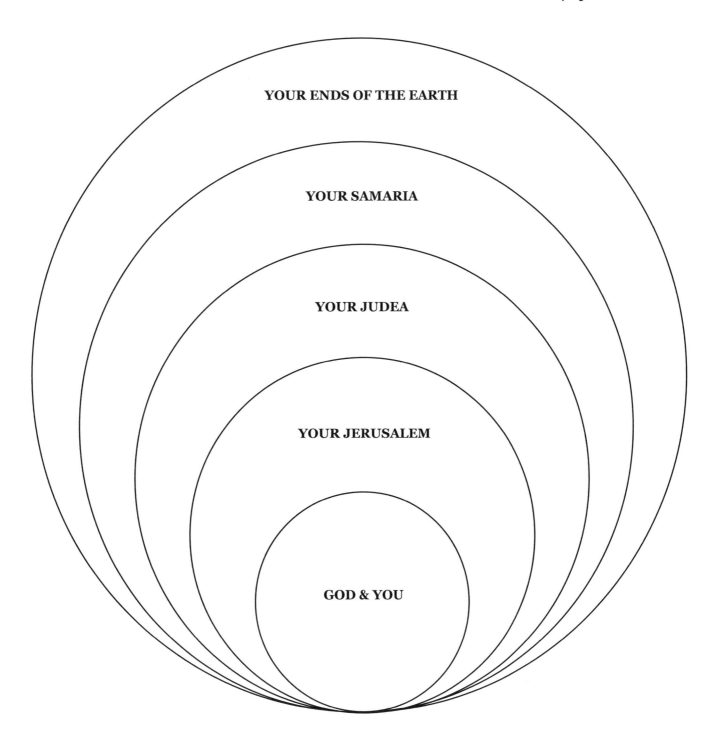

Identify your prayer assignments in light of your insights.

units **1-4** REVIEW & REFLECT

Unit 1 – Worship, Silence and Scripture

Strategy Recap

◆ **Worship is the foundation of all prayer.**
◆ **Stillness is the place we meet with God.**
◆ **Scripture is God's revealed heart to us.**

◆ Which of the three focal points of *Prayer Boot Camp*—**Centrality of Worship**, **Necessity of Stillness** or **Foundation of Scripture**—is most impacting your prayer life? Explain.

◆ How do you see the difference between silence and stillness in your spiritual life?

◆ What specific ideas or tools from this unit are influencing your prayer life?

◆ Do you have any personal experience with the **Going Deeper** exercise you can share?

Unit 2 – Invitation to Relationship

Strategy Recap

Knowing through Scripture who God is, and who we are in Him:

- ◆ **Establishes His authority.**
- ◆ **Reveals our true identity.**
- ◆ **Builds right relationship.**

- ◆ Have Unit 2 materials affected your relationship or intimacy with God? Please explain.

- ◆ How have *Names of God* and *My Identity in Christ* shaped your prayer life?

- ◆ Are there other key points you have gleaned from Unit 2?

- ◆ Do you have any personal experience with the **Going Deeper** exercise you can share?

Unit 3 – Confession and Repentance

Strategy Recap

Confession and Repentance:

- Break agreement with sin and strongholds, leading to freedom.
- Bring redemption, restoration and blessing, evoking gratitude for God's mercy.
- Help us discern conviction, the pathway to confession and repentance.
- Help us discern that condemnation is a dead end leading to bondage.

- Is this view of confession and repentance changing your relationship with God in any way?

- What are the most significant insights you have taken from this unit?

- Has the Lord prompted you to address any areas of unforgiveness in your life?

- Do you have any personal experience with the **Going Deeper** exercise you can share?

Unit 4 – Praying from the Inside Out

Strategy Recap

Inside out prayer:

- **Equips you to express the heart of God in prayer.**
- **Allows your present reality to inform your prayer priority.**
- **Helps you identify your personal prayer assignments.**
- **Releases you from the burden of carrying other people's prayer expectations.**

- In what ways has this unit equipped you to pray from a heart aligned with God's heart?

- Has God reordered your prayer priorities in any way?

- Are there places where God has liberated you from carrying other people's prayer expectations?

- Do you have any personal experience with the **Going Deeper** exercise you can share?

unit 5 PRAYER OF REST

Open with a short prayer welcoming the presence of God and inviting group members to focus their attention on Him.

Allow 5 - 10 minutes for "listening worship" to quiet hearts and minds.

Close worship with a short prayer asking God for revelation as you begin the unit.

Read unit Introduction to the group slowly and clearly, allowing group members to listen and hear.

Worship Suggestions

♦ *Beckon Me* – Mandy Rushing

♦ *You Made a Way* – Matt Gilman

♦ *Carving Out a Place* – Laura Hackett

Recommendation to Facilitator – *Familiarize yourself with the Training Exercise before leading the group. Note that an additional song is suggested as preparation for the exercise.*

Prayer of Rest

At the intersection of our trust and God's unfailing love, we come to the prayer of rest. It is a spiritual oasis in the battlefield, a haven of respite and restoration with God. It is radically different from any place we have been before – in part because it is silent.

Silence is a rare commodity in a mad world. We aren't sure what to do with it. But prayer of rest is less about *doing* than it is about *being*. More about resting than wrestling. More about trusting than striving in the spirit or in the flesh. It is God's gift to our overwrought souls that we may enter His Sabbath rest. "Come. Rest with me. Learn the unforced rhythms of grace."

The prayer of rest is likely to become one of the best loved tools in your prayer arsenal. It trains us to hush the chatter in our heads, and allows our spirits to steep in the presence of God. It reconfigures the landscape of our prayer life by inviting us to climb right up into the lap of our Abba Father and abide in His unfailing love and faithfulness. When we come to the end of ourselves, there is Jesus. He is more than enough. There is nothing we can add to what He has already done on our behalf. We can be fully receptive and utterly still in Him. Selah.

Ask someone to read the Strategy. Continue around the circle taking turns slowly reading aloud and sharing together during the Reflection Questions.

Our identity is 'Beloved of the Lord'. Our battle is to dismiss everything that says otherwise.

Strategy

Prayer of rest is a discipline which invites us to:

- **Silence the chatter so we see and hear only God.**
- **Actively seek and serve God from a posture of rest.**

Centrality of Worship

- Rest is the place where we surrender everything cluttering our hearts and minds, and completely give ourselves over to Jesus Christ. We choose to focus on Him, and determine to hear nothing other than the heartbeat of our Lord. All that remains inside us is the heart cry, "Come Lord Jesus, I want my heart to be your home."

  "This is what the LORD says: 'Heaven is my throne, and the earth is my footstool. Where is the house you will build for me? Where will my resting place be?'" (Isaiah 66:1)

- Prayer of rest is utter submission to the voice and glory of God. God has things He wants to say to us that will be impossible to hear unless we worshipfully rest in Him and prepare a resting place for Him.

  "Guard your steps when you go to the house of God. Go near to listen rather than to offer the sacrifice of fools, who do not know that they do wrong. Do not be quick with your mouth, do not be hasty in your heart to utter anything before God. God is in heaven and you are on earth, so let your words be few. As a dream comes when there are many cares, so the speech of a fool when there are many words." (Ecclesiastes 5:1-3)

- Rest is not a position of our bodies. It is a condition of our hearts.

  "As the deer pants for streams of water, so my soul pants for you, O God. My soul thirsts for God, for the living God. When can I go and meet with God?" (Psalm 42:1-2)

- The heart set at rest is free to worship, regardless of our circumstances.

  "Because you are my help, I sing in the shadow of your wings." (Psalm 63:7)

Reflection Question:

How might you prepare your heart to be a resting place for God's presence?

Read the Reflection Question and allow each person a few moments to respond.

Necessity of Stillness

◆ Our identity is "Beloved of the Lord." Our battle is to dismiss everything that says otherwise.

"Let the beloved of the LORD rest secure in him, for he shields him all day long, and the one the LORD loves rests between his shoulders." (Deuteronomy 33:12)

◆ God's simple invitation is for us as His beloved to rest in His perfect love and grace.

"Are you tired? Worn out? Burned out on religion? Come to me. Get away with me and you'll recover your life. I'll show you how to take a real rest. Walk with me and work with me—watch how I do it. Learn the unforced rhythms of grace. I won't lay anything heavy or ill-fitting on you. Keep company with me and you'll learn to live freely and lightly." (Matthew 11:28-30, The Message)

◆ Our stillness is a measure of our trust in the goodness of God.

"Be at rest once more, O my soul, for the LORD has been good to you." (Psalm 116:7)

Reflection Question:

What comes to mind when you think of "unforced rhythms of grace?"

_____

_____

Foundation of Scripture

◆ Disobedience steals God's rest.

"Today, if you hear his voice, do not harden your hearts as you did at Meribah, as you did that day at Massah in the desert, where your fathers tested and tried me, though they had seen what I did. For forty years I was angry with that generation; I said, 'They are a people whose hearts go astray, and they have not known my ways.' So I declared on oath in my anger, 'They shall never enter my rest.'" (Psalm 95:7-11)

Rest is not a position of our bodies but a condition of our hearts.

Read the Reflection Question and allow each person a few moments to respond.

- The promise of rest is contingent upon obedience and faith.

  "And to whom did God swear that they would never enter his rest if not to those who disobeyed? So we see that they were not able to enter, because of their unbelief." (Hebrews 3:18-19)

- Rest is not a place of inactivity. It is a position of security and right relationship from which we actively seek and serve God.

  "The LORD replied, 'My Presence will go with you, and I will give you rest.'" (Exodus 33:14)

- Rest goes against our natural inclinations. Yet rest equips us to stand in the fullness of God's blessing.

  "In repentance and rest is your salvation, in quietness and trust is your strength, but you would have none of it. Yet the Lord longs to be gracious to you; he rises to show you compassion. For the Lord is a God of Justice. Blessed are all who wait for [rest in] him!" (Isaiah 30:15,18)

- Jesus is the Word of God in human form. He is our resting place. For those who love the Lord and receive His love, the Word is life, rest and refreshment.

  "He makes me lie down in green pastures, he leads me beside quiet waters. He restores my soul." (Psalm 23:2-3)

Reflection Question:

Read the Reflection Question and allow each person a few moments to respond.

Our lives are full of clutter—fear, anxiety, worry, busyness, demands and expectations. How can you experience uncluttered rest in a cluttered world?

_____

_____

Ask someone to read the Strategy Recap.

Strategy Recap

Prayer of rest is a discipline which invites us to:

- **Silence the chatter so we see and hear only God.**
- **Actively seek and serve God from a posture of rest.**

Training

Facilitator: Slowly read the Training Exercise to the group.

"I keep asking that the God of our Lord Jesus Christ, the glorious Father, may give you the Spirit of wisdom and revelation, so that you may know him better." (Ephesians 1:17)

Knowing God through experience and intimacy happens as we take the time to be in His presence. Quiet time spent with the Father conforms and unites us to Christ. When we foster interior silence, we consent to deeper revelation of the Lord.

The Prayer of Rest is a deliberate pause to rest and receive **in silence** as we experience God at a deeper and more intimate level. During the Prayer of Rest we release any expectations, and invite God's presence and action within. The Prayer of Rest is a discipline which may be difficult at first, but grows easier with practice.

Instructions

Preparation:

- Choose a word that is a favorite name or attribute of God. Some examples are *Jesus, Lord, Father, Peace, Holy, Glory, Mercy, Faith, Trust.* Return to this word as a way of refocusing when you become distracted.
- Sit comfortably with eyes closed. Focus your attention on God.

Prayer of Rest:

- Bring your heart and mind to rest in alert stillness before the throne of God.
- Invite the Holy Spirit to help you stay open to the Father.
- Remain silent, releasing all distractions as you surrender to His presence.
- When you become aware of thoughts intruding, let them float by like boats on a river, using your chosen word to help you return to the presence of God.
- Respond to Jesus' invitation in Matthew 11:28—"Come to me, all you who are weary and burdened, and I will give you rest."
- Rest quietly in His presence.

Facilitator:
Quiet hearts and minds by listening to the contemplative worship song before beginning the 20 minute Prayer of Rest. End the quiet time with a short prayer such as: "Father, thank you for this time with you."

SHARE:

- Acknowledge that quieting hearts and minds is a battle.
- Remember that Prayer of Rest is a discipline which will grow easier with practice.
- Share how you experienced this time with the Lord.

Disobedience steals God's rest.

Going Deeper exercises are designed for use in personal quiet time with God between sessions.

Facilitator:
Close with a short prayer or the Lord's Prayer. If time permits you may pray together allowing the unit content and Training to inform your prayers. At the end of Closing Prayer, ask for a volunteer to facilitate the group at the next meeting.

Going Deeper

- ◆ Practice Prayer of Rest daily.

Deeper Still

- ◆ Try extending your time as you are able.
- ◆ Journal about your experience.

unit 6 RECOGNIZING THE VOICE OF GOD

Open with a short prayer welcoming the presence of God and inviting group members to focus their attention on Him.

Allow 5 - 10 minutes for "listening worship" to quiet hearts and minds.

Close worship with a short prayer asking God for revelation as you begin the unit.

Read unit Introduction to the group slowly and clearly, allowing group members to listen and hear.

Worship Suggestions

- *You Made a Way* – Matt Gilman
- *I Am Yours* – Misty Edwards

Recognizing the Voice of God

"My sheep hear my voice." Jesus' declaration urges us to a new level of expectancy in Him. He intends for us to hear His voice! Think of it. We are created with a God-given capacity to commune with Jesus through the Holy Spirit. He expects us to hear and recognize His voice—not just generically but personally. Intimately. The radical truth of our relationship with God is this: not only are we *heard*, but we learn to *hear*. He is training the ears of our hearts to *listen* for the unique voice of our Shepherd-King.

The Word incarnate has a word for us. God's Word speaks to us. Sometimes a verse or phrase from the Bible will come right off the page and into our hearts, as if it is just for us. And it is! Not only does God speak through His Word, first and foremost, but Scripture is also the benchmark for every other message of our Messiah.

Our Shepherd is enormously creative and personal in the ways He speaks to His sheep. Although His voice is seldom audible, God creates in us hearing hearts. As we walk with Him—listening, noticing, expectant—we begin to discern the inner movement and quickening effect of God's voice, the luminous indelibility of His gentle whisper to our hearts. His subtle impartation shimmers with life and resonates with truth in a way that enables us to distinguish God's voice from all the others. And as we obey, we witness the fruit of 'hearing ears.'

Jesus said, "He who belongs to God hears what God says." So, let us pray with Jesus. "He who has ears to hear, let him hear!"

Ask someone to read the Strategy. Continue around the circle taking turns slowly reading aloud and sharing together during the Reflection Questions.

To recognize God's voice is to acknowledge His holiness.

Strategy

To recognize the voice of God:

- ◆ **Expect Him to speak creatively into your life.**
- ◆ **Cultivate a hearing ear attuned to Him.**
- ◆ **Learn to notice His voice in your life and circumstances.**

Centrality of Worship

"Come near to God and he will come near to you." (James 4:8)

- ◆ The key to recognizing God's voice is nearness to Him. He desires nothing more than for us to come to Him in humble adoration. In response, He offers genuine communion through His Holy Spirit.

"Here I am! I stand at the door and knock. If anyone hears my voice and opens the door, I will come in and eat with him, and he with me." (Revelation 3:20)

- ◆ God initiates relationship as we watch and listen for Him in our everyday circumstances. As we draw near in awe and recognition, He speaks to our hearts.

"Now Moses was tending the flock of Jethro his father-in-law, the priest of Midian, and he led the flock to the far side of the desert and came to Horeb, the mountain of God. There the angel of the LORD appeared to him in flames of fire from within a bush. Moses saw that though the bush was on fire it did not burn up. So Moses thought, 'I will go over and see this strange sight—why the bush does not burn up.' When the LORD saw that he had gone over to look, God called to him from within the bush, 'Moses! Moses!' And Moses said, 'Here I am.'" (Exodus 3:1-4)

- ◆ To recognize His voice is to acknowledge His holiness. When we approach Him in a posture of worship, God reveals His identity and purpose.

"'Do not come any closer,' God said. 'Take off your sandals, for the place where you are standing is holy ground.' Then he said, 'I am the God of your father, the God of Abraham, the God of Isaac and the God of Jacob.'" (Exodus 3:5-6)

- ◆ Humility and devotion open the way for us to recognize God's voice and presence in our lives.

"'Do not be afraid, Daniel. Since the first day that you set your mind to gain understanding and to humble yourself before your God, your words were heard, and I have come in response to them.' While he was saying this to me, I bowed with my face toward the ground and was speechless." (Daniel 10:12,15)

◆ The disciplines of worship and fasting invite the Holy Spirit to provide us with clear direction.

"While they were worshiping the Lord and fasting, the Holy Spirit said, 'Set apart for me Barnabas and Saul for the work to which I have called them.'" (Acts 13:2)

Reflection Question:

What do you see as obstacles to recognizing the voice of God in your life?

Read the Reflection Question and allow each person a few moments to respond.

Periods when God seems to be silent are opportunities to build faith in our noise-shattered hearts.

Necessity of Stillness

◆ The practice of inner stillness enables us to recognize the subtle quickening and stirring that characterize God's voice in us. If we are not still, we may miss it.

"When Elizabeth heard Mary's greeting, the baby leaped in her womb, and Elizabeth was filled with the Holy Spirit. 'As soon as the sound of your greeting reached my ears, the baby in my womb leaped for joy.'" (Luke 1:41,44)

◆ Our stillness permits the Father to quiet us with His love. Then we are able to distinguish those places in our lives where He is singing over us.

"The LORD your God is with you, he is mighty to save. He will take great delight in you, he will quiet you with his love, he will rejoice over you with singing." (Zephaniah 3:17)

◆ In dry and trying times it may seem that God is not speaking. Unlike the silent treatment others may use to manipulate us, those periods when God seems to be silent are in truth opportunities to build faith and trust in our noise-shattered hearts. We don't need to fear these times or fill them with something else.

"Therefore I am now going to allure her; I will lead her into the desert and speak tenderly to her." (Hosea 2:14)

◆ Our Father takes great delight in us. Listen for the song that He is singing over you.

"You are my hiding place; you will protect me from trouble and surround me with songs of deliverance." (Psalm 32:7)

Reflection Question:

What is the song you long to hear the Father singing over you?

_____

_____

Read the Reflection Question and allow each person a few moments to respond.

Stillness permits the Father to quiet us with His love.

Foundation of Scripture

"For there is nothing hidden that will not be disclosed, and nothing concealed that will not be known or brought out into the open. Therefore consider carefully how you listen. Whoever has will be given more; whoever does not have, even what he thinks he has will be taken from him." (Luke 8:17-18)

◆ God is constantly speaking to us in many different ways. Our relationship with the Shepherd enables us to distinguish His voice from all the others.

"The man who enters by the gate is the shepherd of his sheep. The watchman opens the gate for him, and the sheep listen to his voice. He calls his own sheep by name and leads them out. When he has brought out all his own, he goes on ahead of them, and his sheep follow him because they know his voice. But they will never follow a stranger; in fact, they will run away from him because they do not recognize a stranger's voice." (John 10:2-5)

◆ Some of the ways God chooses to speak to us:

- **His Word** – "All Scripture is God-breathed and is useful for teaching, rebuking, correcting and training in righteousness, so that the man of God may be thoroughly equipped for every good work." (2 Timothy 3:16-17)

- **His Son, Jesus Christ** – "In the past God spoke to our forefathers through the prophets at many times and in various ways, but in these last days he has spoken to us by his Son, whom he appointed heir of all things, and through whom he made the universe." (Hebrews 1:1-2)

- **His Holy Spirit** – "But God has revealed it to us by his Spirit. The Spirit searches all things, even the deep things of God." (1 Corinthians 2:10)

- **Other People** – "But the Lord said to Ananias, 'Go! This man is my chosen instrument to carry my name before the Gentiles and their kings and before the people of Israel. I will show him how much he must suffer for my name.' Then Ananias went to the house and entered it. Placing his hands on Saul, he said, 'Brother Saul, the Lord—Jesus, who appeared to you on the road as you were coming here—has sent me so that you may see again and be filled with the Holy Spirit.'" (Acts 9:15-17)

- **Creation** – His voice can be seen as well as heard. "For since the creation of the world God's invisible qualities—his eternal power and divine nature—have been clearly seen, being understood from what has been made, so that men are without excuse." (Romans 1:20)

- **Revelation** – "I keep asking that the God of our Lord Jesus Christ, the glorious Father, may give you the Spirit of wisdom and revelation, so that you may know him better. I pray also that the eyes of your heart may be enlightened in order that you may know the hope to which he has called you." (Ephesians 1:17-18)

- **Prophetic Word** – "During this time some prophets came down from Jerusalem to Antioch. One of them, named Agabus, stood up and through the Spirit predicted that a severe famine would spread over the entire Roman world." (Acts 11:27-28)

- **Dreams** – "During the night Paul had a vision of a man of Macedonia standing and begging him, 'Come over to Macedonia and help us.'" (Acts 16:9)

- **Visions** – "One day at about three in the afternoon he had a vision. He distinctly saw an angel of God, who came to him and said, 'Cornelius!'" (Acts 10:3)

- **"God-incidences"** – "Paul and his companions traveled throughout the region of Phrygia and Galatia, having been kept by the Holy Spirit from preaching the word in the province of Asia." (Acts 16:6)

- **Holy Discomfort and Agitation,** in order to move us into a new level of faith – "The LORD had said to Abram, 'Leave your country, your people and your father's household and go to the land I will show you.'" (Genesis 12:1)

- **Testing and Trials** – "Although the Lord gives you the bread of adversity and the water of affliction, your teachers will be hidden no more; with your own eyes you will see them. Whether you turn to the right or to the left, your ears will hear a voice behind you, saying, 'This is the way; walk in it.'" (Isaiah 30:20-21)

We should have an expectation of hearing God's voice.

- ◆ **Desert Seasons**, where He has our complete attention – "Therefore I am now going to allure her; I will lead her into the desert and speak tenderly to her. There I will give her back her vineyards, and will make the Valley of Achor a door of hope. There she will sing as in the days of her youth, as in the day she came up out of Egypt. 'In that day,' declares the LORD, 'you will call me "my husband;" you will no longer call me "my master."'" (Hosea 2:14-16)

- ◆ We should have an expectation of hearing God's voice. If we do not expect, we won't be listening. If we are not listening, we won't hear. If we do not hear, how can we obey? Expectation and obedience foster hearing. Hardness of heart dulls our responsiveness to God.

  "In them is fulfilled the prophecy of Isaiah: 'You will be ever hearing but never understanding; you will be ever seeing but never perceiving. For this people's heart has become calloused; they hardly hear with their ears, and they have closed their eyes. Otherwise they might see with their eyes, hear with their ears, understand with their hearts and turn, and I would heal them.'" (Matthew 13:14-15)

- ◆ God's voice registers in the heart and spirit, as well as in the mind.

  "Then their eyes were opened and they recognized him, and he disappeared from their sight. They asked each other, 'Were not our hearts burning within us while he talked with us on the road and opened the Scriptures to us?'" (Luke 24:31-32)

- ◆ When God speaks it always has power to bring illumination, transformation and life.

  "And God said, 'Let there be light,' and there was light." (Genesis 1:3)

Reflection Question:

In Exodus 20:19 the people asked Moses to listen to God for them.
Who do you go to as a substitute for hearing from God yourself? How does it diminish your ability to hear when you expect from others what you should seek from God?

Read the Reflection Question and allow each person a few moments to respond.

Strategy Recap

To recognize the voice of God:

- **Expect Him to speak creatively into your life.**
- **Cultivate a hearing ear attuned to Him.**
- **Learn to notice His voice in your life and circumstances.**

Ask someone to read the Strategy Recap.

Training

Facilitator: Read.

Discipline of Holy Listening

The Word of God is first and foremost among the ways we hear the Lord in our daily life. The discipline of Holy Listening is designed to help you hear from God in a personal way through Scripture. As you read, **listen** carefully. **Notice** where there is special "movement" or attraction for you in the passage. **Expect** God to speak to you out of His Word.

Take turns reading aloud 2 or 3 times through the following Scripture:

> "There he went into a cave and spent the night. And the word of the LORD came to him: 'What are you doing here, Elijah?' He replied, 'I have been very zealous for the LORD God Almighty. The Israelites have rejected your covenant, broken down your altars, and put your prophets to death with the sword. I am the only one left, and now they are trying to kill me too.' The LORD said, 'Go out and stand on the mountain in the presence of the LORD, for the LORD is about to pass by.' Then a great and powerful wind tore the mountains apart and shattered the rocks before the LORD, but the LORD was not in the wind. After the wind there was an earthquake, but the LORD was not in the earthquake. After the earthquake came a fire, but the LORD was not in the fire. And after the fire came a gentle whisper. When Elijah heard it, he pulled his cloak over his face and went out and stood at the mouth of the cave. Then a voice said to him, 'What are you doing here, Elijah?'" (1 Kings 19:9-13)

Spend 10-15 minutes of silence to reflect on the passage and prompts:

- **Identify** the verse or phrase that stands out to you. Underline it.

- **Reflect** on that verse. Mull it over. How does it speak to you? What significance does it hold for your life?

- **Pray.** Ask God to reveal what He wants to say or show to you. Talk with Him about what is stirred up.

- **Note** any specific suggestion or direction He provides.

- **Rest.** Take a few minutes to be still and thank God for what He has given you.

SHARE with your group what the Lord revealed to you.

Facilitator:
Close with a short prayer or the Lord's Prayer. If time permits you may pray together allowing the unit content and Training to inform your prayers. At the end of Closing Prayer, ask for a volunteer to facilitate the group at the next meeting.

Going Deeper

Have you experienced joy or famine in hearing God speak to your heart?

Going Deeper exercises are designed for use in personal quiet time with God between sessions.

- **Practice** the discipline of Holy Listening in your daily reading of the Word. (Preferably no more than 10 to 15 verses.)

- As you **read**, listen for the verse that draws your attention and stay with it until God offers revelation.

- **Return** to your verse often, speaking it into your circumstances and letting it inform your responses to things that arise throughout the day.

- **Journal** your experience with God in His Word.

The practice of Holy Listening can be used with any portion of Scripture. Here are a few suggested passages to get you started:

- Exodus 3:1-14
- 1 Samuel 3:2-10
- 2 Kings 4:1-7
- Matthew 26:6-13
- Matthew 26:36-46
- Mark 5:25-34
- Luke 5:17-26
- Luke 8:22-25
- John 21:15-19
- 2 Corinthians 3:12-4:1

unit 7 STONES OF REMEMBRANCE

Open with a short prayer welcoming the presence of God and inviting group members to focus their attention on Him.

Allow 5 - 10 minutes for "listening worship" to quiet hearts and minds.

Close worship with a short prayer asking God for revelation as you begin the unit.

Read unit Introduction to the group slowly and clearly, allowing group members to listen and hear.

Worship Suggestions

◆ *I Am Yours* – Misty Edwards
◆ *Jesus Let Me See* – Cory Asbury

Stones of Remembrance

Stones of remembrance are markers on our journey with God to always remind us of His unfailing love and faithfulness. These stones of gratitude are a way of worship as well as a weapon of our warfare.

When God held back the floodwaters of the Jordan so that Israel could cross safely into the Promised Land, He instructed them to carry twelve stones from the dry riverbed to set up on the far side. This altar became a testament and memorial to those who would later ask, "What do these stones mean?"

They meant that future generations could count on God's faithful provision in the face of dire circumstance and humble means. They celebrated the sovereignty and sufficiency of the Father to rescue His people. They remembered the Rock and Redeemer who made a way through the wilderness into the Promised Land.

As Jesus stood at the edge of the river Jordan 1400 years later, he declared, "Out of these stones God can raise up children for Abraham!" And at another place in His journey, when Jesus' disciples were criticized for the boldness of their praise, Jesus said, "If they kept quiet, the stones along the road would burst into cheers!" (Luke 19:40 NLT)

We are His living stones—a declaration of God's faithfulness, a witness to His sovereign power, and a living legacy of His enduring love to future generations. Let us remember with awe and gratitude all that God has done for us!

Ask someone to read the Strategy. Continue around the circle taking turns slowly reading aloud and sharing together during the Reflection Questions.

A grateful heart changes the atmosphere.

Strategy

Intentionally remembering those places where God has met us:

- **Celebrates Him in worship.**
- **Cultivates a grateful heart.**
- **Builds our faith.**
- **Equips us for battle.**

Centrality of Worship

"Enter his gates with thanksgiving and his courts with praise; give thanks to him and praise his name." (Psalm 100:4)

- Praise and thanksgiving honor God and open the gates to His presence.

"Open for me the gates where the righteous enter, and I will go in and thank the Lord. These gates lead to the presence of the Lord, and the godly enter there." (Psalm 118:19-20 NLT)

- Remembering and sharing the goodness of God is a profound expression of worship.

"Then those who feared the LORD talked with each other, and the LORD listened and heard. A scroll of remembrance was written in his presence concerning those who feared the LORD and honored his name." (Malachi 3:16)

- Building altars of remembrance bears witness to God's faithfulness. By intentionally remembering and declaring the goodness of God, we establish a legacy for future generations.

"(Joshua) said to them, 'Go over before the ark of the LORD your God into the middle of the Jordan. Each of you is to take up a stone on his shoulder, according to the number of the tribes of the Israelites, to serve as a sign among you. In the future, when your children ask you, "What do these stones mean?" tell them that the flow of the Jordan was cut off before the ark of the covenant of the LORD. When it crossed the Jordan, the waters of the Jordan were cut off. These stones are to be a memorial to the people of Israel forever.'" (Joshua 4:5-7)

- Marking milestones where God has met us in our journey pays tribute to God's provision for the past. It also builds faith in His promises for the future as we habitually remember what He has done.

"'I am with you, and I will protect you wherever you go. One day I will bring you back to this land. I will not leave you until I have finished giving you everything I have promised you.' Then Jacob awoke from his sleep and said, 'Surely the Lord is in this place, and I wasn't even aware of it!' But he was also afraid and said, 'What an awesome place this is! It is none other than the house of God, the very gateway to heaven!' The next morning Jacob got up very early. He took the stone he had rested his head against, and he set it upright as a memorial pillar. Then he poured olive oil over it. He named that place Bethel (which means "house of God")."
(Genesis 28:15-19 NLT)

Reflection Question:

How might remembering and sharing God's faithfulness with one another be a form of worship?

Read the Reflection Question and allow each person a few moments to respond.

Necessity of Stillness

Christ is the cornerstone for every altar of remembrance we build in the Kingdom.

◆ Stillness provides a pathway for remembrance of God.

"On my bed I remember you; I think of you through the watches of the night. Because you are my help, I sing in the shadow of your wings." (Psalm 63:6-7)

◆ When anxious thoughts arise, revisiting the places where God has been our help allows us to shift from fear to faith.

"Samuel then took a large stone and placed it between the towns of Mizpah and Jeshanah. He named it Ebenezer (which means "the stone of help"), for he said, 'Up to this point the Lord has helped us!'" (1 Samuel 7:12 NLT)

◆ Deliberately remembering the ordinary and extraordinary things God has done for us cultivates a heart of thanksgiving.

"I will remember the deeds of the LORD; yes, I will remember your miracles of long ago. I will meditate on all your works and consider all your mighty deeds."
(Psalm 77:11-12)

◆ These milestones form an altar of communion that reinforces our faith-connection with God.

"Praise the LORD, O my soul, and forget not all his benefits—who forgives all your sins and heals all your diseases, who redeems your life from the pit and crowns you with love and compassion, who satisfies your desires with good things so that your youth is renewed like the eagle's." (Psalm 103:2-5)

◆ A grateful heart changes the atmosphere.

"Finally, brothers, whatever is true, whatever is noble, whatever is right, whatever is pure, whatever is lovely, whatever is admirable—if anything is excellent or praiseworthy—think about such things. . . . And the God of peace will be with you." (Philippians 4:8-9)

Reflection Question:

Describe a time when remembering God's goodness shifted the atmosphere or changed your attitude.

Read the Reflection Question and allow each person a few moments to respond.

_____

_____

Remembering the goodness of God is a profound expression of worship.

Foundation of Scripture

◆ Christ is the cornerstone for every altar of remembrance we build in the kingdom. Return daily to the sure foundation of who He is and what He has done for us.

"See, I lay a stone in Zion, a chosen and precious cornerstone, and the one who trusts in him will never be put to shame." (1 Peter 2:6)

◆ In the Old Testament altars of stone were built in remembrance of God. Today, we as living stones, build altars of remembrance in our hearts where we fellowship with God and receive affirmation of our identity and future.

"The LORD appeared to Abram and said, 'To your offspring I will give this land.' So he built an altar there to the LORD, who had appeared to him. From there he went on toward the hills east of Bethel and pitched his tent, with Bethel on the west and Ai on the east. There he built an altar to the LORD and called on the name of the LORD." (Genesis 12:7-8)

"You also, like living stones, are being built into a spiritual house to be a holy priesthood, offering spiritual sacrifices acceptable to God through Jesus Christ." (1 Peter 2:5)

◆ The altars we build will be visited and revisited by our children and grandchildren. Take care to build altars that glorify God rather than idols that glorify man.

"Only be careful, and watch yourselves closely so that you do not forget the things your eyes have seen or let them slip from your heart as long as you live. Teach them to your children and to their children after them. Remember the day you stood before the LORD your God at Horeb, when he said to me, 'Assemble the people before me to hear my words so that they may learn to revere me as long as they live in the land and may teach them to their children.'" (Deuteronomy 4:9-10)

Remembering what God has done for us cultivates a thankful heart.

- Our remembrances equip us for what is ahead.

"Remember how the LORD your God led you all the way in the desert these forty years, to humble you and to test you in order to know what was in your heart, whether or not you would keep his commands. . . . When you have eaten and are satisfied, praise the LORD your God for the good land he has given you. Be careful that you do not forget the LORD your God, failing to observe his commands, his laws and his decrees that I am giving you this day." (Deuteronomy 8:2,10-11)

- Remembrances are both instruments of worship and weapons of our warfare.

"[David said] 'The LORD who delivered me from the paw of the lion and the paw of the bear will deliver me from the hand of this Philistine. . . .' Then he took his staff in his hand, chose five smooth stones from the stream, put them in the pouch of his shepherd's bag and, with his sling in his hand, approached the Philistine. . . . 'You come against me with sword and spear and javelin, but I come against you in the name of the LORD Almighty, the God of the armies of Israel, whom you have defied.'" (1 Samuel 17:37,40,45)

- Circumstances can overwhelm us. Remembering how God has met us in hard places renews our hope and trust in Him.

"I remember my affliction and my wandering, the bitterness and the gall. I well remember them, and my soul is downcast within me. Yet this I call to mind and therefore I have hope: Because of the LORD's great love we are not consumed, for his compassions never fail. They are new every morning; great is your faithfulness." (Lamentations 3:19-23)

- God is worthy of our thanks and praise regardless of our circumstances.

"Be joyful always; pray continually; give thanks in all circumstances, for this is God's will for you in Christ Jesus." (1 Thessalonians 5:16-18)

Read the Reflection Question and allow each person a few moments to respond.

Reflection Question:

Is there a specific memory of God's faithfulness that helps you face trying times?

_____

_____

Ask someone to read the Strategy Recap.

Strategy Recap

Intentionally remembering those places where God has met us:

- ◆ **Celebrates Him in worship.**
- ◆ **Cultivates a grateful heart.**
- ◆ **Builds our faith.**
- ◆ **Equips us for battle.**

Training

Facilitator: Allow 15 - 20 minutes of silence for group members to do the following training. At the end of the reflection time, invite the group to share what God is showing them.

TimeLine Exercise

In Acts 7 Stephen offers a detailed account of God's faithfulness to Israel. His remembrance is his defense. His testimony points to the altars of grace and defining moments in Israel's journey with God.

Your character has been formed and defined largely by what we call 'critical incidents,' not least of which are those places where God has met you.

This **TimeLine exercise** invites you to reflect on these markers and milestones in order to discern more clearly God's hand and working in your life.

Reflect on defining moments with God on your journey.

Consider places where God has:

- ◆ Guided you through spiritual transition
- ◆ Spoken into your life
- ◆ Provided for your need
- ◆ Intervened in your circumstance
- ◆ Comforted you in pain
- ◆ Helped you through adversity
- ◆ Healed you or someone you love
- ◆ Called you to a new level of faith

Using the TimeLine on the next page marked from Birth to Present, choose a word or symbol to mark each place as a *stone* of recognition and remembrance.

Thank Him for these specific points of grace in your journey.

SHARE with your group what God is showing you.

Return to this exercise throughout the week, asking God to reveal stones of remembrance you may have overlooked.

Birth

Present

Facilitator:
Close with a short prayer or the Lord's Prayer. If time permits you may pray together allowing the unit content and Training to inform your prayers. At the end of Closing Prayer, ask for a volunteer to facilitate the group at the next meeting.

Going Deeper

◆ Keep this TimeLine in mind as you continue your journey with God.

◆ Fill in your TimeLine with other key events, turning points, transitions, decisions and relationships. It may be helpful to journal specifics of these defining moments.

◆ Reflect on how God has used these 'critical incidents' to shape your life, character and faith journey. Talk with God about their significance.

◆ Ask for the healing or release you may still need from any of these events.

◆ Thank Him for these specific points of grace in your journey.

Going Deeper exercises are designed for use in personal quiet time with God between sessions.

unit 8 PRAYING LIKE THE BRIDE, NOT THE WIDOW

Worship Suggestions

- *Jesus Let Me See* – Cory Asbury
- *Favorite One* – Misty Edwards

Praying Like the Bride, Not the Widow

In this unit, the widow and the Bride are descriptive not of marital status, but the condition of our hearts in relationship to Jesus Christ, the heavenly Bridegroom. Do we approach the throne of grace with worshipful abandon or apathy? Confident trust or doubt? Spiritual abundance or poverty? Intimacy or barrenness?

The identifying characteristics of the Bride and the widow struggle for supremacy in our lives and in our churches. We must battle for our Bridehood—breaking free from the grave clothes and shame the enemy uses to tarnish our true status as the Beloved and Betrothed of Christ.

For all eternity, God has chosen, set apart and purposed the Body of Christ for her role as the Bride at the Wedding Feast of the Lamb. Until then, we make ourselves ready for that day.

Ask someone to read the Strategy. Continue around the circle taking turns slowly reading aloud and sharing together during the Reflection Questions.

Prayer is an expression of our intimacy with Christ.

Strategy

- **Delight in God's desire for you, His Bride.**
- **You are in covenant relationship with God— all His promises are yours.**
- **You have authority and favor in Christ, the Bridegroom.**

Centrality of Worship

"By day the LORD directs his love, at night his song is with me—a prayer to the God of my life." (Psalm 42:8)

- As a groom woos his bride, so Christ draws us to Himself. From the foundations of the world, our marriage to Christ, the Bridegroom, has been arranged. We rejoice in Him who has loved us from the beginning.

"I have loved you with an everlasting love; I have drawn you with loving-kindness." (Jeremiah 31:3)

"Though you have not seen him, you love him; and even though you do not see him now, you believe in him and are filled with an inexpressible and glorious joy." (1 Peter 1:8)

- The Bible begins with a wedding in the Garden of Eden and ends with the Wedding Supper of the Lamb. Everything in between is the divine love story of God's preparation of His church as the Bride for His beloved Son.

"Praise the Lord! For the Lord our God, the Almighty, reigns. Let us be glad and rejoice, and let us give honor to him. For the time has come for the wedding feast of the Lamb, and his bride has prepared herself. She has been given the finest of pure white linen to wear. For the fine linen represents the good deeds of God's holy people." (Revelation 19:6-8 NLT)

- Just as a bride has eyes only for her groom, so are we made to be fascinated and enthralled with God.

"Who is this that appears like the dawn, fair as the moon, bright as the sun, majestic as the stars in procession?" (Song of Songs 6:10)

"The LORD is exalted over all the nations, his glory above the heavens. Who is like the LORD our God, the One who sits enthroned on high, who stoops down to look on the heavens and the earth?" (Psalm 113:4-6)

◆ The Bride longs to be where the Bridegroom is. In His presence, she is fulfilled.

"You have made known to me the path of life; you will fill me with joy in your presence, with eternal pleasures at your right hand." (Psalm 16:11)

◆ In becoming human, Christ forever joined Himself to us. As the Bridegroom, His desire is that we become one with Him and delight that He has secured our place and position as His Bride.

"Father, I desire those you have given me to be with me where I am. Then they will see my glory, which you have given me because you loved me before the world's foundation." (John 17:24 Holman CSB)

◆ Aligning with the authority of Christ positions us to pray as His Bride. His desires become our desires, the two becoming one.

"'In that day,' declares the LORD,' you will call me "my husband;" you will no longer call me "my master. . . ." I will betroth you to me forever; I will betroth you in righteousness and justice, in love and compassion. I will betroth you in faithfulness, and you will acknowledge the LORD.'" (Hosea 2:16,19-20)

Reflection Question:

"My lover is mine and I am his." (Song of Songs 2:16). Pause and savor this. In what ways have you been fascinated by God?

Necessity of Stillness

◆ The human heart yearns for true love. As the Bride of Christ, our hearts crave and thirst for intimacy with God.

"As the deer pants for streams of water, so my soul pants for you, O God. My soul thirsts for God, for the living God. When can I go and meet with God?" (Psalm 42:1-2)

◆ Wherever you are, wherever God takes you, He has prepared a place of intimacy and abundance where His Spirit resides in you.

When the Church learns to pray like His Bride, the world will see God the way He is meant to be seen.

Read the Reflection Question and allow each person a few moments to respond.

"You hem me in—behind and before; you have laid your hand upon me. Such knowledge is too wonderful for me, too lofty for me to attain. Where can I go from your Spirit? Where can I flee from your presence? If I go up to the heavens, you are there; if I make my bed in the depths, you are there. If I rise on the wings of the dawn, if I settle on the far side of the sea, even there your hand will guide me, your right hand will hold me fast." (Psalm 139:5-10)

- Intimacy with God liberates our hearts to respond in love to His pure delight in us.

"You have stolen my heart, my sister, my bride; you have stolen my heart with one glance of your eyes, with one jewel of your necklace. How delightful is your love, my sister, my bride!" (Song of Songs 4:9-10)

- Covenant marriage speaks to the mystery of the union between Christ and His church.

"Husbands, love your wives, just as Christ loved the church and gave himself up for her to make her holy, cleansing her by the washing with water through the word, and to present her to himself as a radiant church, without stain or wrinkle or any other blemish, but holy and blameless. . . . 'For this reason a man will leave his father and mother and be united to his wife, and the two will become one flesh.' This is a profound mystery—but I am talking about Christ and the church." (Ephesians 5:25-27, 31-32)

- You are the Bride of Christ. Rest in who God says you are.

"The nations will see your righteousness. World leaders will be blinded by your glory. And you will be given a new name by the Lord's own mouth. The Lord will hold you in his hand for all to see—a splendid crown in the hand of God. Never again will you be called 'The Forsaken City' or 'The Desolate Land.' Your new name will be 'The City of God's Delight' and 'The Bride of God,' for the Lord delights in you and will claim you as his bride. Your children will commit themselves to you, O Jerusalem, just as a young man commits himself to his bride. Then God will rejoice over you as a bridegroom rejoices over his bride." (Isaiah 62:2-5 NLT)

Reflection Question:

Read the Reflection Question and allow each person a few moments to respond.

How do you respond to the thought of delighting in God or God delighting in you?

_____

_____

Foundation of Scripture

♦ The Father has chosen us to be the Bride. He never abandons us—even when we are unfaithful—and He never leaves us widowed. His heart for the widow is to make her His Bride.

"Do not be afraid; you will not suffer shame. Do not fear disgrace; you will not be humiliated. You will forget the shame of your youth and remember no more the reproach of your widowhood. For your Maker is your husband—the LORD Almighty is his name—the Holy One of Israel is your Redeemer; he is called the God of all the earth." (Isaiah 54:4-5)

♦ The Bride and the widow are descriptive not of marital status, but the condition of our hearts in relationship to Christ.

"If you have any encouragement from being united with Christ, if any comfort from his love, if any fellowship with the Spirit, if any tenderness and compassion, then make my joy complete by being like-minded, having the same love, being one in spirit and purpose." (Philippians 2:1-2)

♦ Intimate relationship with God carries us from widow to Bride through His unbreakable covenant of love. It is our choice to receive abundant identity in Christ or succumb to widowhood.

"All praise to God, the Father of our Lord Jesus Christ, who has blessed us with every spiritual blessing in the heavenly realms because we are united with Christ. Even before he made the world, God loved us and chose us in Christ to be holy and without fault in his eyes. God decided in advance to adopt us into his own family by bringing us to himself through Jesus Christ. This is what he wanted to do, and it gave him great pleasure. So we praise God for the glorious grace he has poured out on us who belong to his dear Son. He is so rich in kindness and grace that he purchased our freedom with the blood of his Son and forgave our sins. He has showered his kindness on us, along with all wisdom and understanding." (Ephesians 1:3-8 NLT)

♦ God Himself provides the dowry for His Bride. The Bride price is paid in full by the very blood of Christ. Our authority as Christ's Bride is rooted in our intimacy with Him.

"Since we have confidence to enter the Most Holy Place by the blood of Jesus, by a new and living way opened for us through the curtain, that is, his body, and since we have a great priest over the house of God, let us draw near to God with a sincere heart in full assurance of faith, having our hearts sprinkled to cleanse us from a guilty conscience and having our bodies washed with pure water." (Hebrews 10:19-22)

> The Bride's intimacy with God determines her capacity to intimidate the enemy.

We are made to be fascinated with God.

- Once we say "I do," all the promises of God belong to us in Christ Jesus. Under His authority and protection God's Kingdom is available to us.

  "For the Son of God, Jesus Christ, who was preached among you by me and Silas and Timothy, was not 'Yes' and 'No,' but in him it has always been 'Yes.' For no matter how many promises God has made, they are 'Yes' in Christ. And so through him the 'Amen' is spoken by us to the glory of God." (2 Corinthians 1:19-20)

- Out of this relationship, prayer becomes an expression of our intimacy and alignment with Christ rather than a religious performance or ritual. His faithfulness enables us to exercise spiritual authority out of His abundance rather than our poverty.

  "God also bound himself with an oath, so that those who received the promise could be perfectly sure that he would never change his mind. So God has given both his promise and his oath. These two things are unchangeable because it is impossible for God to lie. Therefore, we who have fled to him for refuge can have great confidence as we hold to the hope that lies before us. This hope is a strong and trustworthy anchor for our souls. It leads us through the curtain into God's inner sanctuary." (Hebrews 6:17-19 NLT)

- There is no sense of entitlement in the prayer of the Bride. On the contrary, she approaches God with humble confidence and absolute trust, as a beneficiary of the Father's faithfulness to His Son, our Bridegroom. This is the battle position of the Bride from which she exercises true spiritual authority.

  "And I will do whatever you ask in my name, so that the Son may bring glory to the Father. You may ask me for anything in my name, and I will do it." (John 14:13-14)

  "Which of you, if his son asks for bread, will give him a stone? Or if he asks for a fish, will give him a snake? If you, then, though you are evil, know how to give good gifts to your children, how much more will your Father in heaven give good gifts to those who ask him!" (Matthew 7:9-11)

- The Bride is able to weather seasons of adversity and mourning by leaning on her Bridegroom.

  "Who is this coming up from the desert leaning on her lover?" (Song of Songs 8:5)

  "You turned my wailing into dancing; you removed my sackcloth and clothed me with joy." (Psalm 30:11)

- The Bride's intimacy with God determines her capacity to intimidate the enemy.

"He who dwells in the shelter of the Most High will rest in the shadow of the Almighty. I will say of the LORD, 'He is my refuge and my fortress, my God, in whom I trust. . . .' You will tread upon the lion and the cobra; you will trample the great lion and the serpent. 'Because he loves me,' says the LORD, 'I will rescue him; I will protect him, for he acknowledges my name.'" (Psalm 91:1-2, 13-14)

◆ When the church learns to pray like His Bride, the world will see God the way He is meant to be seen.

"And we, who with unveiled faces all reflect the Lord's glory, are being transformed into his likeness with ever-increasing glory, which comes from the Lord, who is the Spirit." (2 Corinthians 3:18)

◆ In the union between the Bride and the Bridegroom, there is no separation, no divorce, no widowhood.

"Never will I leave you; never will I forsake you." (Hebrews 13:5)

"Take me away with you—let us hurry! Let the king bring me into his chambers." (Song of Songs 1:4)

"Come, I will show you the bride, the wife of the Lamb." (Revelation 21:9)

Reflection Question:

In what ways do you see intimacy with God as a weapon against the enemy?

_____

_____

Read the Reflection Question and allow each person a few moments to respond.

Strategy Recap

◆ **Delight in God's desire for you, His Bride.**
◆ **You are in covenant relationship with God—
   all His promises are yours.**
◆ **You have authority and favor in Christ, the Bridegroom.**

Ask someone to read the Strategy Recap.

Training

Facilitator: Allow 15-20 minutes of silence for group members to do the following training. At the end of the reflection time, invite the group to share what God is showing them.

Tarry quietly with the Lord.

Reflect on the following passage from Psalm 27:4-6.

> "One thing I ask of the LORD, this is what I seek:
>> that I may dwell in the house of the LORD all the days of my life,
>> to gaze upon the beauty of the LORD and to seek him in his temple.
> For in the day of trouble he will keep me safe in his dwelling;
>> he will hide me in the shelter of his tabernacle and set me high upon a rock.
> Then my head will be exalted above the enemies who surround me;
>> at his tabernacle will I sacrifice with shouts of joy;
>> I will sing and make music to the LORD."

Consider this passage and other portions of Unit 8. What do you see as hallmarks and attributes of the Bride? How do you understand characteristics of the widow?

List some of these below.

Bride	Widow
Example: I have eyes for you only, Jesus.	*Example: I can't see past my own circumstances.*

How do you perceive yourself as you come before God in prayer? Do you have the confident expectancy of the Bride? Do you plead and bargain like a widow?

Ask the Holy Spirit to draw you into deeper intimacy with the Lord.

Rest in your identity as the Bride of Christ.

SHARE what God is showing you.

Facilitator:
Close with a short prayer or the Lord's Prayer. If time permits you may pray together allowing the unit content and Training to inform your prayers. At the end of Closing Prayer, ask for a volunteer to facilitate the group at the next meeting.

Going Deeper

Read aloud Psalms 42 and 43. (In the Hebrew text they are one psalm.)

Identify the language of Bridehood and the language of widowhood within this prayer for deliverance.

Going Deeper exercises are designed for use in personal quiet time with God between sessions.

Prayer of the Bride

Prayer of the Widow

Translate these expressions into your own terminology or prayer language.

Exercise your "Bride language" in talking with the Lord about your present need and longings.

units 5-8 REVIEW & REFLECT

Unit 5 – Prayer of Rest

Strategy Recap

Prayer of rest is a discipline which invites us to:

- **Silence the chatter so we see and hear only God.**
- **Actively seek and serve God from a posture of rest.**

- How has the Prayer of Rest changed your devotional experience with God?

- How has practicing this posture of rest affected your willingness to trust in and surrender to God? Please explain.

- What other points or ideas in Unit 5 are impacting your daily life?

- Do you have any personal experience with the **Going Deeper** exercise you can share?

Unit 6 – Recognizing the Voice of God

Strategy Recap

To recognize the voice of God:

♦ Expect Him to speak creatively into your life.
♦ Cultivate a hearing ear attuned to Him.
♦ Learn to notice His voice in your life and circumstances.

♦ How has this unit affected your awareness of hearing God's voice?

♦ How is expectancy and attentiveness to God's voice changing your relationship with Him?

♦ How is hearing from God affecting your prayer life and other relationships?

♦ Do you have any personal experience with the **Going Deeper** exercise you can share?

Unit 7 – Stones of Remembrance

Strategy Recap

Intentionally remembering those places where God has met us:

- ◆ **Celebrates Him in worship.**
- ◆ **Cultivates a grateful heart.**
- ◆ **Builds our faith.**
- ◆ **Equips us for battle.**

◆ How has this unit encouraged you to deliberately recognize, celebrate and give thanks to God as you remember the places He has met you?

◆ How might you share your "stones of remembrance" with the generations that precede and follow yours?

◆ Which of the truths and blessings in this unit do you desire to impart to your family?

◆ How does remembering what God has done equip you for battle?

◆ Do you have any personal experience with the **Going Deeper** exercise you can share?

Unit 8 – Praying Like the Bride, Not the Widow

Strategy Recap

- Delight in God's desire for you, His Bride.
- You are in covenant relationship with God— all His promises are yours.
- You have authority and favor in Christ, the Bridegroom.

- How has delighting in God's desire for you affected your intimacy with Him?

- How is knowing your identity and authority as Christ's Bride changing your prayer life?

- All His promises are yours. Which of the promises in Unit 8 are you appropriating in your prayer life?

- Do you have any personal experience with the **Going Deeper** exercise you can share?

unit 9 AT THE KING'S TABLE

Open with a short prayer welcoming the presence of God and inviting group members to focus their attention on Him.

Allow 5 - 10 minutes for "listening worship" to quiet hearts and minds.

Close worship with a short prayer asking God for revelation as you begin the unit.

Read unit Introduction to the group slowly and clearly, allowing group members to listen and hear.

Worship Suggestions

♦ *Favorite One* – Misty Edwards
♦ *You Satisfy* – Julie Meyer

At The King's Table

God in His infinite love has always provided a table for His people, a feasting place of spiritual plenty and provision. From the manna in the desert and the bread of presence set within the ark of covenant, to the coming of Jesus Christ the Bread of Life and the new wine of His Holy Spirit, God invites us to a progressive feast of abundance that will culminate with the wedding feast of the Lamb at His return.

As Psalm 23 reminds us, God's table is ever set before us in the very presence of our enemies. Lies, distractions and substitutes keep us from the lavish spiritual provision of our King. As His children, heirs and priests, we partake of His spiritual manna as a matter of discipline and delight, trusting God's provision without yielding to the distraction or intimidation of the enemy.

God's Spirit and His Word invite us to reach beyond our natural boundaries to our supernatural blessedness at the place Jesus holds for us by grace at His Father's table.

Come – taste and see that the Lord is good!

Ask someone to read the Strategy. Continue around the circle taking turns slowly reading aloud and sharing together during the Reflection Questions.

We always need to consider where we are feasting.

Strategy

- **Come with confidence to the King's Table.**
- **Be assured of the place set for you.**
- **Partake and be satisfied in His bountiful provision.**

Centrality of Worship

"He has taken me to the banquet hall, and his banner over me is love."
(Song of Songs 2:4)

- God's love is our ever-present resource. To enter His banqueting hall is to receive the grace and plenty of Christ.

- God is most glorified in us when we are most satisfied in Him.

"Come, all you who are thirsty, come to the waters; and you who have no money, come, buy and eat! Come, buy wine and milk without money and without cost. Why spend money on what is not bread, and your labor on what does not satisfy? Listen, listen to me, and eat what is good, and your soul will delight in the richest of fare."
(Isaiah 55:1-2)

- Rejoice! We feast on the abundance of Jesus in whom we have the bread of life, the wine of the new covenant and the ministry of the Holy Spirit.

"They will come and shout for joy on the heights of Zion; they will rejoice in the bounty of the LORD—the grain, the new wine and the oil, the young of the flocks and herds. They will be like a well-watered garden, and they will sorrow no more."
(Jeremiah 31:12)

- The feast of God's unfailing love and provision for His people turns our mourning to dancing and our darkness to light.

"'Then maidens will dance and be glad, young men and old as well. I will turn their mourning into gladness; I will give them comfort and joy instead of sorrow. I will satisfy the priests with abundance, and my people will be filled with my bounty,' declares the LORD." (Jeremiah 31:13-14)

"How priceless is your unfailing love! Both high and low among men find refuge in the shadow of your wings. They feast on the abundance of your house; you give them drink from your river of delights. For with you is the fountain of life; in your light we see light." (Psalm 36:7-9)

Reflection Question:

Picture yourself at the Lord's banquet. What does the table look like?

Read the Reflection Question and allow each person a few moments to respond.

Necessity of Stillness

"The LORD is my shepherd, I shall not be in want." (Psalm 23:1)

- Rest in the Lord as your Shepherd. Follow His lead. His path of righteousness is our path of restoration.

"He makes me lie down in green pastures, he leads me beside quiet waters, he restores my soul. He guides me in paths of righteousness for his name's sake." (Psalm 23:2-3)

- The press of trying circumstances always surrounds us. As we fix our gaze on the Shepherd, His presence, provision and protection become our ultimate reality.

"Even though I walk through the valley of the shadow of death, I will fear no evil, for you are with me; your rod and your staff, they comfort me." (Psalm 23:4)

- God has set a table for us in the presence of our enemies. Sometimes we don't go to the table because all we see is the enemy. Stillness shifts our gaze back to the table set with goodness and love by the Lord.

"You prepare a table before me in the presence of my enemies. You anoint my head with oil; my cup overflows. Surely goodness and love will follow me all the days of my life, and I will dwell in the house of the LORD forever." (Psalm 23:5-6)

- Just as a shepherd watches over his flock and cares for their every need, so the Lord is watching over you and providing for your every need.

"The LORD is my shepherd, I shall not be in want." (Psalm 23:1)

God is most glorified in us when we are most satisfied in Him.

Reflection Question:

What draws you to or keeps you from the King's table?

Read the Reflection Question and allow each person a few moments to respond.

Foundation of Scripture

"Here I am! I stand at the door and knock. If anyone hears my voice and opens the door, I will come in and eat with him, and he with me." (Revelation 3:20)

◆ Earnest seekers and recipients of divine grace gather at the King's table to discuss matters closest to His heart, and to receive direction and sustenance for the day. We approach the table by grace, and by grace He holds a place for us there.

"From the fullness of his grace we have all received one blessing after another." (John 1:16)

◆ Only by the power of the Holy Spirit can we partake of the Father's feast. Through His power, revelation and understanding we are transformed in Christ.

"I keep asking that the God of our Lord Jesus Christ, the glorious Father, may give you the Spirit of wisdom and revelation, so that you may know him better. I pray also that the eyes of your heart may be enlightened in order that you may know the hope to which he has called you, the riches of his glorious inheritance in the saints, and his incomparably great power for us who believe." (Ephesians 1:17-19)

God invites us to a progressive feast of abundance.

◆ The King's table is set with a glorious feast which strengthens us to walk in victory, authority and spiritual provision in Christ. Consider the following items on the banquet menu:

- ◆ **Mercy and Grace** – "Let us then approach the throne of grace with confidence, so that we may receive mercy and find grace to help us in our time of need." (Hebrews 4:16)

- ◆ **Love** – "And so we know and rely on the love God has for us. God is love." (1 John 4:16)

- ◆ **Forgiveness** – "For he has rescued us from the dominion of darkness and brought us into the kingdom of the Son he loves, in whom we have redemption, the forgiveness of sins." (Colossians 1:13-14)

- ◆ **Salvation** – "Blessed be the Lord, who daily loads us with benefits, the God of our salvation! Selah." (Psalm 68:19 NKJV)

- ◆ **Adoption** – ". . . he predestined us to be adopted as his sons through Jesus Christ, in accordance with his pleasure and will." (Ephesians 1:5)

- ◆ **Holy Spirit Power** – "But you will receive power when the Holy Spirit comes on you; and you will be my witnesses in Jerusalem, and in all Judea and Samaria, and to the ends of the earth." (Acts 1:8)

- **His Name** – ". . . I kneel before the Father, from whom his whole family in heaven and on earth derives its name." (Ephesians 3:14-15)

- **Transformation** – "Therefore, if anyone is in Christ, he is a new creation; the old has gone, the new has come!" (2 Corinthians 5:17)

- **Identity** – "But you are a chosen people, a royal priesthood, a holy nation, a people belonging to God, that you may declare the praises of him who called you out of darkness into his wonderful light." (1 Peter 2:9)

- **Purpose** – "For we are God's workmanship, created in Christ Jesus to do good works, which God prepared in advance for us to do." (Ephesians 2:10)

- **Authority** – "I have given you authority to trample on snakes and scorpions and to overcome all the power of the enemy; nothing will harm you." (Luke 10:19)

- **Victory** – "'At my table you will eat your fill of horses and riders, mighty men and soldiers of every kind,' declares the Sovereign LORD." (Ezekiel 39:20)

- **Crown of Life** – "Blessed is the man who perseveres under trial, because when he has stood the test, he will receive the crown of life that God has promised to those who love him." (James 1:12)

- **The Kingdom of God** – ". . . has not God chosen those who are poor in the eyes of the world to be rich in faith and to inherit the kingdom he promised those who love him?" (James 2:5)

- **His Promises** – "The LORD is faithful to all his promises and loving toward all he has made." (Psalm 145:13)

- **Provision** – "His divine power has given us everything we need for life and godliness through our knowledge of him who called us by his own glory and goodness." (2 Peter 1:3)

- **Faith** – "For it is by grace you have been saved, through faith—and this not from yourselves, it is the gift of God . . ." (Ephesians 2:8)

- **Peace** – "Peace I leave with you; my peace I give you. I do not give to you as the world gives. Do not let your hearts be troubled and do not be afraid." (John 14:27)

- **Wisdom** – "If any of you lacks wisdom, he should ask God, who gives generously to all without finding fault, and it will be given to him." (James 1:5)

◆ **Righteousness** – ". . . be found in him, not having a righteousness of my own that comes from the law, but that which is through faith in Christ—the righteousness that comes from God and is by faith." (Philippians 3:9)

◆ **Freedom** – "It is for freedom that Christ has set us free. Stand firm, then, and do not let yourselves be burdened again by a yoke of slavery." (Galatians 5:1)

◆ **Armor** – "Therefore put on the full armor of God, so that when the day of evil comes, you may be able to stand your ground, and after you have done everything, to stand." (Ephesians 6:13)

◆ **Equipping** – "All Scripture is God-breathed and is useful for teaching, rebuking, correcting and training in righteousness, so that the man of God may be thoroughly equipped for every good work." (2 Timothy 3:16-17)

◆ **Revelation** – "I keep asking that the God of our Lord Jesus Christ, the glorious Father, may give you the Spirit of wisdom and revelation, so that you may know him better." (Ephesians 1:17)

◆ **Gifts and Calling** – ". . . for God's gifts and his call are irrevocable." (Romans 11:29)

◆ **His Word** – "Jesus answered, 'It is written: "Man does not live on bread alone, but on every word that comes from the mouth of God."'" (Matthew 4:4)

◆ **Strategies** – "The LORD is my rock, my fortress and my deliverer; my God is my rock, in whom I take refuge. He is my shield and the horn of my salvation, my stronghold. I call to the LORD, who is worthy of praise, and I am saved from my enemies." (Psalm 18:2-3)

◆ **The Bread of His Presence** – "Give us today our daily bread." (Matthew 6:11)

◆ **Bread of Life** – "Then Jesus declared, 'I am the bread of life. He who comes to me will never go hungry, and he who believes in me will never be thirsty.'" (John 6:35)

◆ **The Bread of Adversity** – "Yet the LORD longs to be gracious to you; he rises to show you compassion. . . . As soon as he hears, he will answer you. Although the Lord gives you the bread of adversity and the water of affliction, your teachers will be hidden no more; with your own eyes you will see them. Whether you turn to the right or to the left, your ears will hear a voice behind you, saying, 'This is the way; walk in it.'" (Isaiah 30:18-21)

◆ **The Cup of Suffering** – "But rejoice that you participate in the sufferings of Christ, so that you may be overjoyed when his glory is revealed." (1 Peter 4:13)

- **Communion** – "While they were eating, Jesus took bread, gave thanks and broke it, and gave it to his disciples, saying, 'Take and eat; this is my body.' Then he took the cup, gave thanks and offered it to them, saying, 'Drink from it, all of you. This is my blood of the covenant, which is poured out for many for the forgiveness of sins.'" (Matthew 26:26-28)

- **Eternity** – "On this mountain the LORD Almighty will prepare a feast of rich food for all peoples, a banquet of aged wine—the best of meats and the finest of wines. On this mountain he will destroy the shroud that enfolds all peoples, the sheet that covers all nations; he will swallow up death forever." (Isaiah 25:6-8)

- The King has invited you to partake of the lavish feast at His banquet table.

  "Taste and see that the LORD is good; blessed is the man who takes refuge in him." (Psalm 34:8)

- We always need to consider where we are feasting.

  "You cannot drink the cup of the Lord and the cup of demons too; you cannot have a part in both the Lord's table and the table of demons." (1 Corinthians 10:21)

Reflection Question:

Are you receiving spiritual nourishment from the King's table, or soulish junk food from somewhere else?

_____

_____

Strategy Recap

- **Come with confidence to the King's Table.**
- **Be assured of the place set for you.**
- **Partake and be satisfied in His bountiful provision.**

Come – taste and see that the Lord is good!

Read the Reflection Question and allow each person a few moments to respond.

Ask someone to read the Strategy Recap.

Training

Facilitator: Allow 15-20 minutes of silence for group members to do the following training. At the end of the reflection time, invite the group to share what God is showing them.

Imagine yourself approaching the King's Table. A chair awaits you. Sit and be still.

Spend a few minutes imagining the table. The setting. The feast set before you.
Stay quietly with this picture for a few minutes.

When you are ready, turn to the 'menu' of provisions found in **Foundation of Scripture**.

Make notes as you go through the list, asking yourself the following questions about each item:

- ◆ Where are you feasting?

- ◆ Where are you skimping? Why?

Reflect:

- ◆ Where are your most active places of craving or desire? Depletion?

- ◆ Talk with the Father about your longings.

- ◆ Ask Him what else might be on the King's Table for you.

SHARE with your group what God is showing you.

Facilitator:
Close with a short prayer or the Lord's Prayer. If time permits you may pray together allowing the unit content and Training to inform your prayers. At the end of Closing Prayer, ask for a volunteer to facilitate the group at the next meeting.

Going Deeper

Going Deeper exercises are designed for use in personal quiet time with God between sessions.

Jesus said, "To those who overcome I will give some of the hidden manna and a white stone with a new name known only to the one who receives it." (Revelation 2:17) This is the present-future reality of believers in the world today who press through trying times and circumstances to partake of God's hidden manna—the spiritual provision, revelation and sustenance we have in Jesus Christ, the Bread of Life. And what of the white stone?

In ancient times, it was traditional to offer honored guests a white stone with a secret name or message for their eyes only. Olympic athletes were awarded white stones inscribed with their personal achievement and prize. The stone was also used as a token giving its bearer access to special events, celebrations and feasts. For Christians, the white stone is our place holder at His Kingdom table that identifies us as His own, carrying attributes and authority belonging to Christ.

The wedding banquet is ready! The King awaits your presence.

Meditate on Revelation 2:17 in light of the King's table.

Reflect on the significance of the hidden manna and the white stone Jesus promises His overcomers.

Write the King a message of personal acceptance and thanksgiving for the table He has set before you and the place He has provided for you there.

Ask God daily to lead you to the fullness of His feasting place.

unit 10 THE BATTLE READY WARRIOR

Open with a short prayer welcoming the presence of God and inviting group members to focus their attention on Him.

Allow 5 - 10 minutes for "listening worship" to quiet hearts and minds.

Close worship with a short prayer asking God for revelation as you begin the unit.

Read unit Introduction to the group slowly and clearly, allowing group members to listen and hear.

Worship Suggestions

- *You Satisfy* – Julie Meyer
- *I Put on Christ* – Laura Hackett

The Battle Ready Warrior

Everything leading up to this unit of *Prayer Boot Camp* is preparation for the Battle Ready Warrior. As we learn to walk in right relationship and identity in Jesus—praising His name, trusting His provision, exercising the authority of His Word—we grow in readiness for the battle that rages around us and against us.

What is that battle? Satan is out to undermine and defeat our faith at every turn. He has aimed a flood of iniquity against the people of God. He will stop at nothing to diminish the name of Jesus and the Christ-likeness of those who bear it.

The enemy uses the shiny things of the material world to mask the invisible reality of this battle for our souls. But we stand ready. We see Jesus. We choose Christ. And from Him we receive the weapons of our warfare and the safe-haven of His invincibility.

Fear not! Our victory is assured in Christ alone who trains our hands for battle and our hearts for war!

Ask someone to read the Strategy. Continue around the circle taking turns slowly reading aloud and sharing together during the Reflection Questions.

Strategy

- **Recognize that there is an all-out war from the enemy on the identity, authority and purity of the name of Jesus.**
- **Recognize that there is an all-out assault by the enemy on the identity, authority, purity and destiny of God's people.**
- **Know that our God is the Lord of heaven's armies. He is the One who equips, trains and leads us into battle.**
- **Prepare for war!**

The battle ready warrior stays close to his Commander-in-Chief.

Centrality of Worship

"Let them give glory to the LORD and proclaim his praise . . . The LORD will march out like a mighty man, like a warrior he will stir up his zeal; with a shout he will raise the battle cry and will triumph over his enemies." (Isaiah 42:12-13)

- The warrior Bride follows her heavenly Commander-in-Chief—the LORD God Almighty is His name.

"Who is this King of glory? The LORD strong and mighty, the LORD mighty in battle." (Psalm 24:8)

- We are the Lord's army. The battle belongs to Him and so do we. Let us boldly lift our voice in praise to Him who makes us ready for war.

"Praise be to the LORD my Rock, who trains my hands for war, my fingers for battle." (Psalm 144:1)

- Worship and the Word prepare us for battle.

"Let the high praises of God be in their mouth, and a two-edged sword in their hand." (Psalm 149:6 NKJV)

Reflection Question:

How might worship stir up the warrior's zeal in us?

Read the Reflection Question and allow each person a few moments to respond.

_____

_____

We stand ready.
We see Jesus. We
choose Christ.

Necessity of Stillness

◆ We war from a place of intimacy and authority, hidden with God.

"For you are my hiding place; you protect me from trouble. You surround me with songs of victory." (Psalm 32:7 NLT)

◆ We find our defense in Christ, standing firm in the knowledge that God is our fortress in the midst of turmoil. In stillness, His provision and protection are absolute.

"Find rest, O my soul, in God alone; my hope comes from him. He alone is my rock and my salvation; he is my fortress, I will not be shaken." (Psalm 62:5-6)

◆ The Battle Ready Warrior engages stillness as a vital weapon.

"The LORD will fight for you; you need only to be still." (Exodus 14:14)

◆ As we dwell in Him, God Himself is our covering and shield in battle.

"He will cover you with His feathers, and under His wings you will find refuge; His faithfulness will be your shield and rampart. You will not fear the terror of night, nor the arrow that flies by day." (Psalm 91:4-5)

Reflection Question:

What is the source of your defense? How can stillness be an asset on the battlefield?

_____

_____

Read the Reflection Question and allow each person a few moments to respond.

Foundation of Scripture

"It is God who arms me with strength and makes my way perfect. He makes my feet like the feet of a deer; he enables me to stand on the heights. He trains my hands for battle; my arms can bend a bow of bronze." (Psalm 18:32-34)

◆ Satan is hell-bent on destroying God's people. We concede ground to him when we fail to recognize this.

"The thief comes only to steal and kill and destroy; I have come that they may have life, and have it to the full." (John 10:10)

◆ Our circumstances and the people around us are not the enemy.

"For our struggle is not against flesh and blood, but against the rulers, against the authorities, against the powers of this dark world and against the spiritual forces of evil in the heavenly realms." (Ephesians 6:12)

We war from a place of intimacy and authority, hidden with God.

◆ God has provided us with His full armor to protect, equip and identify us as His warriors.

"Finally, be strong in the Lord and in his mighty power. Put on the full armor of God so that you can take your stand against the devil's schemes. . . . Therefore put on the full armor of God, so that when the day of evil comes, you may be able to stand your ground, and after you have done everything, to stand." (Ephesians 6:10-11; 13)

◆ Each piece of God's armor for us is represented in the person of Jesus Christ:

  ◆ **The Belt of Truth** – Jesus is our Truth. "Jesus answered, 'I am the way and the truth and the life. No one comes to the Father except through me.'" (John 14:6)

  ◆ **The Breastplate of Righteousness** – Jesus is our Righteousness. "God made him who had no sin to be sin for us, so that in him we might become the righteousness of God." (2 Corinthians 5:21)

  ◆ **Sandals of the Readiness of the Gospel of Peace** – Jesus is the good news and our Prince of Peace. "For God was pleased to have all his fullness dwell in him, and through him to reconcile to himself all things, whether things on earth or things in heaven, by making peace through his blood, shed on the cross." (Colossians 1:19-20)

  ◆ **Shield of Faith** – Jesus is the author and perfecter of our faith. "Let us fix our eyes on Jesus, the author and perfecter of our faith, who for the joy set before him endured the cross, scorning its shame, and sat down at the right hand of the throne of God." (Hebrews 12:2)

  ◆ **Helmet of Salvation** – Jesus crowns us with His salvation. "Salvation is found in no one else, for there is no other name under heaven given to men by which we must be saved." (Acts 4:12)

  ◆ **Sword of the Spirit** – The Word of God is the sword of the Spirit and Jesus is the living Word. "The Word became flesh and made his dwelling among us. We have seen his glory, the glory of the One and Only . . . " (John 1:14)

  ◆ **Pray in the Spirit** – Prayer is the battle. "And pray in the Spirit on all occasions with all kinds of prayers and requests. With this in mind, be alert and always keep on praying for all the saints." (Ephesians 6:18)

"Stand firm then, with the belt of truth buckled around your waist, with the breastplate of righteousness in place, and with your feet fitted with the readiness that comes from the gospel of peace. In addition to all this, take up the shield of faith, with which you can extinguish all the flaming arrows of the evil one. Take the helmet of salvation and the sword of the Spirit, which is the word of God." (Ephesians 6:14-17)

◆ **As the Battle Ready Warrior:**

- ◆ **Have the mind of Christ** – "Do not conform any longer to the pattern of this world, but be transformed by the renewing of your mind. Then you will be able to test and approve what God's will is—His good, pleasing and perfect will." (Romans 12:2)

- ◆ **Fear the Lord** – "The fear of the LORD is the beginning of knowledge . . . " (Proverbs 1:7)

- ◆ **Ask God for wisdom** –"If any of you lacks wisdom, he should ask God, who gives generously to all without finding fault, and it will be given to him." (James 1:5)

- ◆ **Know how to order the day** – "In the morning, O LORD, you hear my voice; in the morning I lay my requests before you and wait in expectation." (Psalm 5:3)

- ◆ **Be kind, compassionate and forgiving** – "Be kind and compassionate to one another, forgiving each other, just as in Christ God forgave you." (Ephesians 4:32)

- ◆ **Edify others with your words** – "Do not let any unwholesome talk come out of your mouths, but only what is helpful for building others up according to their needs, that it may benefit those who listen." (Ephesians 4:29)

- ◆ **Have peace, trusting in God** – "Do not let your hearts be troubled. Trust in God; trust also in Me." (John 14:1)

- ◆ **Resist the enemy** – "Be self-controlled and alert. Your enemy the devil prowls around like a roaring lion looking for someone to devour. Resist him, standing firm in the faith, because you know that your brothers throughout the world are undergoing the same kind of sufferings." (1 Peter 5:8-9)

- ◆ **Abstain from sinful desires** – "Dear friends, I urge you, as aliens and strangers in the world, to abstain from sinful desires, which war against your soul." (1 Peter 2:11)

Worship and the Word prepare us for battle.

- **Put off the old nature** – "Put to death, therefore, whatever belongs to your earthly nature: sexual immorality, impurity, lust, evil desires and greed, which is idolatry. . . . But you must rid yourselves of all such things as these: anger, rage, malice, slander, and filthy language from your lips. Do not lie to each other . . . " (Colossians 3:5, 8-9)

- **Put on the new self** – ". . . you have taken off your old self with its practices and have put on the new self, which is being renewed in knowledge in the image of its Creator. . . . Therefore, as God's chosen people, holy and dearly loved, clothe yourselves with compassion, kindness, humility, gentleness and patience." (Colossians 3:9-10, 12)

- **Count worldly credentials worthless compared to your identity in Christ** – "But whatever was to my profit I now consider loss for the sake of Christ." (Philippians 3:7)

- **Know that God and heaven's armies are with you** – "When the servant of the man of God got up and went out early the next morning, an army with horses and chariots had surrounded the city. 'Oh, my lord, what shall we do?' the servant asked. 'Don't be afraid,' the prophet answered. 'Those who are with us are more than those who are with them.' And Elisha prayed, 'O LORD, open his eyes so he may see.' Then the LORD opened the servant's eyes, and he looked and saw the hills full of horses and chariots of fire all around Elisha." (2 Kings 6:15-17)

- **Fix your eyes on eternity, trusting in the finished work of God** – "Therefore, we do not lose heart. Though outwardly we are wasting away, yet inwardly we are being renewed day by day. For our light and momentary troubles are achieving for us an eternal glory that far outweighs them all. So we fix our eyes not on what is seen, but on what is unseen. For what is seen is temporary, but what is unseen is eternal." (2 Corinthians 4:16-18)

- **Do not give place to the devil** – ". . . and do not give the devil a foothold." (Ephesians 4:27)

- **Do not grieve the Holy Spirit** – "And do not grieve the Holy Spirit of God, with whom you were sealed for the day of redemption." (Ephesians 4:30)

- **Do not quench the Holy Spirit** – "Do not put out the Spirit's fire; do not treat prophecies with contempt. Test everything. Hold on to the good. Avoid every kind of evil." (1 Thessalonians 5:19-22)

- **Do not use worldly weapons to fight spiritual battles** – "For though we live in the world, we do not wage war as the world does. The weapons we fight with are not the weapons of the world. On the contrary, they have divine power to demolish strongholds." (2 Corinthians 10:3-4)

◆ Alert to every scheme of the enemy, the Battle Ready Warrior stays close to his Commander-in-Chief.

"The Lord of Heaven's Armies is here among us; the God of Israel is our fortress." (Psalm 46:11 NLT)

"Watch and pray so that you will not fall into temptation. The spirit is willing, but the body is weak." (Matthew 26:41)

Reflection Question:

Do you have perceptions or attitudes that need to shift in order to be battle-ready?

_____

_____

Read the Reflection Question and allow each person a few moments to respond.

Strategy Recap

◆ **Recognize that there is an all-out war from the enemy on the identity, authority and purity of the name of Jesus.**
◆ **Recognize that there is an all-out assault by the enemy on the identity, authority, purity and destiny of God's people.**
◆ **Know that our God is the Lord of heaven's armies. He is the One who equips, trains and leads us into battle.**

Ask someone to read the Strategy Recap.

Ask someone to read For Clarity.

For Clarity

Belt of Truth	Jesus is our Truth.
Breastplate of Righteousness	Jesus is our Righteousness.
Sandals of the Readiness of the Gospel of Peace	Jesus is the good news and our Prince of Peace.
Shield of Faith	Jesus is the author and perfecter of our faith.
Helmet of Salvation	Jesus crowns us with His salvation.
Sword of the Spirit	Jesus is the living Word.

PRACTICE DAILY PUTTING ON CHRIST, THE FULL ARMOR OF GOD.

Training

Facilitator: Allow 15-20 minutes of silence for group members to do the following training. At the end of the reflection time, invite the group to share what God is showing them.

Consider each piece of the armor of God.

◆ What does it cover?

◆ What does it protect you from?

◆ Where are you most vulnerable?

SHARE with your group what God is revealing to you.

Going Deeper exercises are designed for use in personal quiet time with God between sessions.

Going Deeper

Consider the attributes of the Battle Ready Warrior.

- ◆ Where do you feel prepared?

- ◆ Where do you feel unprepared?

Ask the Lord to upgrade your battle readiness and journal any direction you receive for developing the Battle Ready Warrior in you.

unit 11 THE OVERCOMING WARRIOR

Worship Suggestions

- *I Put on Christ* – Laura Hackett
- *Conquering Lion* – Grace Falkner

The Overcoming Warrior

Sound the Shofar! Muster my forces, for the battle is at hand.

Though the enemy try to steal your intimacy, kill your identity and destroy your authority in Christ, take heart! The Lord is near. He will save, redeem and restore all things in Christ so that you may have victorious life and have it to the full.

Stand on your true identity in Jesus.
Contend for your intimacy in Him.
War for your peace.
Battle for unity in the Spirit and holy zeal in your faith.

Behold! The Lord comes with a two-edged sword in His mouth to fight for your freedom from the enemy's taunting, temptation and tyranny. All strength, authority and victory belong to Jesus.

The outcome of this battle? Beloved, it isn't even close.

No weapon forged against you will prosper when the King of Glory fights for you. So, do not allow yourself to be conformed to the mindset of the material world, but instead be transformed by His Word. Then **you** become the SWORD in his hand, a spiritual weapon in his arsenal!

"I will . . . make you like a Warrior's Sword." (Zechariah 9:13)

Ask someone to read the Strategy. Continue around the circle taking turns slowly reading aloud and sharing together during the Reflection Questions.

The King of Glory fights for you.

Strategy

- ◆ **Seek God's strategy for your battle.**
- ◆ **Hold your God-given position.**
- ◆ **Fix your hope on His victory, not on the rubble.**
- ◆ **Exercise the authority of His Word.**
- ◆ **Trust God to fight for you.**

Centrality of Worship

<u>Battle Strategy in Worship from 2 Chronicles 20</u>

◆ Our resolve to seek and inquire of the Lord establishes us in a strategic posture of worship.

"Alarmed, Jehoshaphat resolved to inquire of the LORD, and he proclaimed a fast for all Judah. The people of Judah came together to seek help from the LORD . . ." (2 Chronicles 20:3-4)

◆ Standing firm in the presence of God is our declaration that His power, might, and holy name are able to deliver us.

"O LORD, God of our fathers, are you not the God who is in heaven? You rule over all the kingdoms of the nations. Power and might are in your hand, and no one can withstand you. If calamity comes upon us, whether the sword of judgment, or plague or famine, we will stand in your presence before this temple that bears your Name and will cry out to you in our distress, and you will hear us and save us." (2 Chronicles 20:6, 9)

◆ Humility is at the heart of worship.

"O our God, will you not judge them? For we have no power to face this vast army that is attacking us. We do not know what to do, but our eyes are upon you." (2 Chronicles 20:12)

◆ God has specific strategies He desires to reveal. Remain steadfast in confidence that the battle belongs to the Lord. Take your position in worship. Receive His direction. Obey!

"This is what the LORD says to you: 'Do not be afraid or discouraged because of this vast army. For the battle is not yours, but God's. You will not have to fight this battle. Take up your positions; stand firm and see the deliverance the LORD will give you . . . Do not be afraid; do not be discouraged. Go out to face them tomorrow, and the LORD will be with you.'" (2 Chronicles 20:15, 17)

◆ Our God and His strategies are awesome! Respond to Him with worshipful abandon in whatever way the Spirit moves you.

"Jehoshaphat bowed with his face to the ground, and all the people of Judah and Jerusalem fell down in worship before the LORD. Then some Levites from the Kohathites and Korahites stood up and praised the LORD, the God of Israel, with very loud voice." (2 Chronicles 20:18-19)

◆ Trusting God's strategy is both worship and warfare.

"Listen to me, Judah and people of Jerusalem! Have faith in the LORD your God and you will be upheld; have faith in his prophets and you will be successful." (2 Chronicles 20:20)

◆ Worship is the leading edge of His strategy for our victory.

"After consulting the people, Jehoshaphat appointed men to sing to the LORD and to praise him for the splendor of his holiness as they went out at the head of the army, saying: 'Give thanks to the LORD, for his love endures forever.'" (2 Chronicles 20:21)

◆ Worship displaces fear, doubt and unbelief. While we praise, God fights for us.

"As they began to sing and praise, the LORD set ambushes against the men of Ammon and Moab and Mount Seir who were invading Judah, and they were defeated." (2 Chronicles 20:22)

◆ Worship and obedience enable us to plunder the enemy camp and take back what rightly belongs to the Kingdom of God.

"So Jehoshaphat and his men went to carry off their plunder, and they found among them a great amount of equipment and clothing and also articles of value—more than they could take away. There was so much plunder that it took three days to collect it. On the fourth day they assembled in the Valley of Beracah [Praise], where they praised the LORD." (2 Chronicles 20:25-26)

◆ Effective battle strategies begin and end with praise.

"Then, led by Jehoshaphat, all the men of Judah and Jerusalem returned joyfully to Jerusalem, for the LORD had given them cause to rejoice over their enemies. They entered Jerusalem and went to the temple of the LORD with harps and lutes and trumpets." (2 Chronicles 20:27-28)

Reflection Question:

Picture yourself plundering the defeated enemy camp. What are you reclaiming?

_____

_____

Read the Reflection Question and allow each person a few moments to respond.

Effective battle strategies begin and end with praise.

Necessity of Stillness

Battle Strategy in Stillness from The Lord's Prayer

◆ Prayer is a heart-to-heart transaction between us and our Father. Close the door on anything that disrupts or distorts communion with Him.

"But when you pray, go into your room, close the door and pray to your Father, who is unseen. Then your Father, who sees what is done in secret, will reward you." (Matthew 6:6)

◆ Sometimes our words are the very thing that keeps us from heart-to-heart communion with Him.

"And when you pray, do not keep on babbling like pagans, for they think they will be heard because of their many words. Do not be like them, for your Father knows what you need before you ask him." (Matthew 6:7-8)

◆ Jesus instructs us, "This, then, is how you should pray." (Matthew 6:9)

◆ My Father is sovereign and His name is holy.

"Our Father in heaven, hallowed be your name . . ." (Matthew 6:9)

◆ My Father's strategy advances His Kingdom here on earth.

". . . your kingdom come, your will be done on earth as it is in heaven." (Matthew 6:10)

- My Father's supply provides for my every need.

    "Give us today our daily bread." (Matthew 6:11)

- My Father forgives me and requires that I forgive others in the same way.

    "Forgive us our debts, as we also have forgiven our debtors."
    (Matthew 6:12)

- My Father hides me from the enemy and plans my deliverance.

    "And lead us not into temptation, but deliver us from the evil one."
    (Matthew 6:13)

- Rest in the knowledge that your Father's prayer strategy is complete.

"Yours is the kingdom and the power and the glory forever. Amen."
(Matthew 6:13 NKJV)

Reflection Question:

How do you see forgiveness as a strategic weapon? How might unforgiveness compromise your identity as the Overcoming Warrior?

_____

_____

Read the Reflection Question and allow each person a few moments to respond.

Foundation of Scripture

<u>Battle Strategy in Scripture from Nehemiah 3 and 4</u>

- Fellowship and unity are key battle strategies. The Bible states twenty-one times in Nehemiah 3 that the builders repairing the walls of Jerusalem worked <u>next to</u> each other.

"*Next to* them, Zadok son of Immer made repairs opposite his house. *Next to* him, Shemaiah son of Shecaniah, the guard at the East Gate, made repairs." (Nehemiah 3:29 *Italics Added*) (See Nehemiah 3:2-31)

- Scripture sets forth multiple battle strategies for the Overcoming Warrior. Consider the battle tactics in Nehemiah 4:

  - Recognize mockery and ridicule as tools of the opposition and turn them back on the enemy through prayer.

Worship and obedience enable us to plunder the enemy camp.

The outcome of
this battle?
Beloved, it isn't
even close.

"When Sanballat heard that we were rebuilding the wall, he became angry and was greatly incensed. He ridiculed the Jews, and in the presence of his associates and the army of Samaria, he said, 'What are those feeble Jews doing?' Hear us, O our God, for we are despised. Turn their insults back on their own heads. Give them over as plunder in a land of captivity." (Nehemiah 4:1-2, 4)

♦ Persevere wholeheartedly.

"So we rebuilt the wall till all of it reached half its height, for the people worked with all their heart." (Nehemiah 4:6)

♦ Understand that prayer and vigilance provide your protection.

"They all plotted together to come and fight against Jerusalem and stir up trouble against it. But we prayed to our God and posted a guard day and night to meet this threat." (Nehemiah 4:8-9)

♦ Refuse to be intimidated by rubble, ruin or threat. Rally the family of God to stand with you and take up assigned positions to strengthen places of weakness and exposure.

"Meanwhile, the people in Judah said, 'The strength of the laborers is giving out, and there is so much rubble that we cannot rebuild the wall.' Also our enemies said, 'Before they know it or see us, we will be right there among them and will kill them and put an end to the work.' Then the Jews who lived near them came and told us ten times over, 'Wherever you turn, they will attack us.' Therefore I stationed some of the people behind the lowest points of the wall at the exposed places, posting them by families, with their swords, spears and bows." (Nehemiah 4:10-13)

♦ Assess the battlefield, remembering the Lord's faithfulness above all else. Contend for the inheritance that rightly belongs to the family of God.

"After I looked things over, I stood up and said to the nobles, the officials and the rest of the people, 'Don't be afraid of them. Remember the Lord, who is great and awesome, and fight for your brothers, your sons and your daughters, your wives and your homes.'" (Nehemiah 4:14)

♦ Remain focused, always returning to your assigned work, trusting in God to deal with your enemies.

"When our enemies heard that we were aware of their plot and that God had frustrated it, we all returned to the wall, each to his own work." (Nehemiah 4:15)

♦ Stand ready for battle whether you are working, watching, supporting or supplying. Carry your work and weapons at the same time, always armed with the sword—the Word of God.

"From that day on, half of my men did the work, while the other half were equipped with spears, shields, bows and armor. The officers posted themselves behind all the people of Judah who were building the wall. Those who carried materials did their work with one hand and held a weapon in the other, and each of the builders wore his sword at his side as he worked." (Nehemiah 4:16-18)

♦ Realize your strength is in unity and respond quickly to the call to gather. In this place God fights for you.

"But the man who sounded the trumpet stayed with me. Then I said . . . 'The work is extensive and spread out, and we are widely separated from each other along the wall. Wherever you hear the sound of the trumpet, join us there. Our God will fight for us!'" (Nehemiah 4:18-20)

♦ Do not give in to slumber and complacency. Know where you are supposed to be and when you are supposed to be there.

"So we continued the work with half the men holding spears, from the first light of dawn till the stars came out. At that time I also said to the people, 'Have every man and his helper stay inside Jerusalem at night, so they can serve us as guards by night and workmen by day.'" (Nehemiah 4:21-22)

♦ Never take off your armor or lay down your weapon in the midst of battle.

"Neither I nor my brothers nor my men nor the guards with me took off our clothes; each had his weapon, even when he went for water." (Nehemiah 4:23)

- Battle strategies in the Kingdom of God are neither formula nor finite. The Overcoming Warrior stays close to the Father, always listening for His plans and tactics.

"I will listen to what God the LORD will say; he promises peace to his people, his saints . . ." (Psalm 85:8)

Reflection Question:

Read the Reflection Question and allow each person a few moments to respond.

Can you identify the rubble, ruin or threat that keeps you from being the Overcoming Warrior?

_____

_____

Ask someone to read the Strategy Recap.

Strategy Recap

- ◆ **Seek God's strategy for your battle.**
- ◆ **Hold your God-given position.**
- ◆ **Fix your hope on His victory, not on the rubble.**
- ◆ **Exercise the authority of His Word.**
- ◆ **Trust God to fight for you.**

Training

Facilitator: Allow 15-20 minutes of silence for group members to do the following training. At the end of the reflection time, invite the group to share what God is showing them.

> "He made my mouth like a sharpened sword, in the shadow of his hand he hid me;
> he made me into a polished arrow and concealed me in his quiver." (Isaiah 49:2)

Look back at the strategies of the Overcoming Warrior. Ask God to identify some of the shifts you need to make in order to gain strategic advantage in spiritual battle.

How is God inviting you to upgrade your understanding and practice of effective strategies for the victorious warrior in terms of:

◆ Worship

◆ Stillness

◆ Scripture

What specific strategies do you need to apply for the battle you are facing? Ask God to show you.

SHARE with your group what the Lord is revealing to you.

Going Deeper exercises are designed for use in personal quiet time with God between sessions.

Facilitator:
Close with a short prayer or the Lord's Prayer. If time permits you may pray together allowing the unit content and Training to inform your prayers. At the end of Closing Prayer, ask for a volunteer to facilitate the group at the next meeting.

Going Deeper

Read and reflect on:

♦ 2 Chronicles 20

♦ Matthew 6:9-13

♦ Nehemiah 3-4

Note verses that God wants to give you for strategic advancement.

Apply the sharp edge of His Word to your present battleground.

unit 12 BEHOLDING GOD

Worship Suggestions

◆ *Holy* – Matt Gilman
◆ *My Beloved* – Cory Asbury

Beholding God

We become what we behold! This is the source and secret of our spiritual transformation.

The ministry of beholding is the genesis and foundation for all other ministry in the Kingdom. As we set our gaze on Christ, cherishing every facet and feature of His presence, our hearts are changed into the very likeness of that which we behold. Saturated with Jesus, streams of living water begin to flow—though we ourselves may not perceive the transformation. For "where our treasure is, there will our hearts be also."

As Jesus becomes the anchor for all that we hold dear and treasure in our hearts, the Spirit cultivates in us a keen discernment of spiritual things. Ardent seekers and avid students of the true, the genuine and the authentic will recognize the sham, the fraud and the counterfeit. Nothing less than Christ will do. His presence changes us because we are abiding in the vine of the Beloved.

To behold is also to be held. Fixing the gaze of our hearts on the person of Jesus—in His suffering and in His glory—we experience the joy and freedom of belonging. We are the apple of His eye and the delight of His heart, as we delight ourselves in Him. And steeping in His presence, we reflect the radiance of His glory and the light of His countenance to shine into the dark places of the world.

Ask someone to read the *Strategy*. Continue around the circle taking turns slowly reading aloud and sharing together during the *Reflection Questions*.

Strategy

- ◆ **Be saturated in His presence through worship.**
- ◆ **Behold the Father through the Son.**
- ◆ **Be transformed by His love.**
- ◆ **Become His love to others.**

We become what we behold.

Centrality of Worship

"Looking at Jesus as He walked, he said, 'Behold the Lamb of God!'"
(John 1:36 NKJV)

- ◆ You created us to be loved and be held by You. Seeing Your face captivates our hearts.

"One thing I ask of the LORD, this is what I seek: that I may dwell in the house of the LORD all the days of my life, to gaze on the beauty of the LORD and to seek him in his temple. My heart says of you, 'Seek his face!' Your face, LORD, I will seek. I am still confident of this: I will see the goodness of the LORD in the land of the living." (Psalm 27:4,8,13)

- ◆ We long for Your presence in our lives. Having beheld You, we are ruined for anything less. Nothing satisfies our souls like Your love.

"O God, you are my God, earnestly I seek you; my soul thirsts for you, my body longs for you, in a dry and weary land where there is no water. I have seen you in the sanctuary and beheld your power and your glory. Because your love is better than life, my lips will glorify you." (Psalm 63:1-3)

- ◆ Beholding You, O God, is our ultimate worship and highest praise. We have no greater ministry than to reflect Your glory.

"And we, who with unveiled faces all reflect the Lord's glory, are being transformed into his likeness with ever-increasing glory, which comes from the Lord, who is the Spirit. . . . Therefore, since through God's mercy we have this ministry, we do not lose heart." (2 Corinthians 3:18;4:1)

"As for me, I will see Your face in righteousness; I shall be satisfied when I awake in Your likeness." (Psalm 17:15 NKJV)

Reflection Question:

Pause and consider what it means to behold God. What comes to mind?

Read the Reflection Question and allow each person a few moments to respond.

_____

_____

Necessity of Stillness

"John saw Jesus coming toward him, and said, 'Behold! The Lamb of God who takes away the sin of the world!'" (John 1:29 NKJV)

Our capacity to be stilled is our capacity to be filled.

♦ Stillness opens our hearts to behold You. In that private sanctuary You invite us to draw near.

"Therefore, brothers and sisters, since we have confidence to enter the Most Holy Place by the blood of Jesus, by a new and living way opened for us through the curtain, that is, his body, and since we have a great priest over the house of God, let us draw near to God with a sincere heart." (Hebrews 10:19-22)

♦ Your death forever removed the veil of separation between us.

"But whenever anyone turns to the Lord, the veil is taken away. Now the Lord is the Spirit, and where the Spirit of the Lord is, there is freedom." (2 Corinthians 3:16-17)

♦ Our capacity to be stilled is our capacity to be filled.

   ♦ Father, as we behold You, we receive Your extravagant love through Jesus.

   "As the Father has loved me, so have I loved you. Now remain in my love." (John 15:9)

   ♦ Father, as we behold You, we begin to know You because of Your Son.

   "Now this is eternal life: that they may know you, the only true God, and Jesus Christ, whom you have sent." (John 17:3)

   ♦ Father, as we behold You, we rejoice in the gift of belonging to You through Jesus.

   "I will not leave you as orphans; I will come to you. Before long, the world will not see me anymore, but you will see me. Because I live, you also will live. On that day you will realize that I am in my Father, and you are in me, and I am in you." (John 14:18-20)

- Father, as we behold You, we abide in Your abundance through Christ.

  "I am the vine; you are the branches. If a man remains in me and I in him, he will bear much fruit; apart from me you can do nothing." (John 15:5)

- Father, as we behold You, we rest in Your perfect peace through Christ.

  "Peace I leave with you; my peace I give you. I do not give to you as the world gives. Do not let your hearts be troubled and do not be afraid." (John 14:27)

- Father, as we behold You, we grow in unity to give glory to Your name.

  "I have given them the glory that you gave me, that they may be one as we are one: I in them and you in me. May they be brought to complete unity to let the world know that you sent me and have loved them even as you have loved me." (John 17:22-23)

- Father, as we behold You, we look forward to the place You have prepared for us through Jesus.

  "Do not let your hearts be troubled. Trust in God; trust also in me. In my Father's house are many rooms; if it were not so, I would have told you. I am going there to prepare a place for you. And if I go and prepare a place for you, I will come back and take you to be with me that you also may be where I am." (John 14:1-3)

- Father, as we behold You, we delight in being with You where Jesus is.

  "Father, I want those you have given me to be with me where I am, and to see my glory, the glory you have given me because you loved me before the creation of the world." (John 17:24)

- The more time we spend in stillness with You, the more healing it becomes. Our quiet reverence and receptivity allow You to touch and transform places deep inside that cannot be healed any other way.

  "But for you who revere my name, the sun of righteousness will rise with healing in its wings. And you will go out and leap like calves released from the stall." (Malachi 4:2)

Reflection Question:

How might you experience transformation or healing in your practice of beholding God?

_____

_____

Foundation of Scripture

"'Behold, the Lion of the tribe of Judah, the Root of David, has prevailed . . .' And I looked, and behold, in the midst of the throne and of the four living creatures, and in the midst of the elders, stood a Lamb as though it had been slain." (Revelation 5:5-6 NKJV)

Jesus longs for the hospitality of an undivided heart.

◆ We must behold You in Your suffering before we can behold You in Your glory.

"But we have this treasure in jars of clay to show that this all-surpassing power is from God and not from us. We are hard pressed on every side, but not crushed; perplexed, but not in despair; persecuted, but not abandoned; struck down, but not destroyed. We always carry around in our body the death of Jesus, so that the life of Jesus may also be revealed in our body." (2 Corinthians 4:7-10)

◆ We will not allow our focus to be fixed on our present circumstance but on You, our hope of glory.

"For our light and momentary troubles are achieving for us an eternal glory that far outweighs them all. So we fix our eyes not on what is seen, but on what is unseen, since what is seen is temporary, but what is unseen is eternal." (2 Corinthians 4:17-18)

◆ Those whose faces shine with Your reflected glory have paid a price. We trust You to transform our suffering into that which will bring glory to You.

"Now if we are children, then we are heirs—heirs of God and co-heirs with Christ, if indeed we share in his sufferings in order that we may also share in his glory. I consider that our present sufferings are not worth comparing with the glory that will be revealed in us." (Romans 8:17-18)

◆ The more we die to ourselves, the greater our capacity to bring Your life to others.

"In this you greatly rejoice, though now for a little while you may have had to suffer grief in all kinds of trials. These have come so that your faith—of greater worth than gold, which perishes even though refined by fire—may be proved genuine and may result in praise, glory and honor when Jesus Christ is revealed." (1 Peter 1:6-7)

◆ As Your children we rejoice that we are more than we could be on our own, but not yet all that we are becoming.

"Dear friends, now we are children of God, and what we will be has not yet been made known. But we know that when Christ appears, we shall be like him, for we shall see him as he is." (1 John 3:2)

Beholding You, we are ruined for anything less.

Read the Reflection Question and allow each person a few moments to respond.

Ask someone to read the Strategy Recap.

◆ We will love one another, Father, in order to please you, to make You known, and to reflect Your glory.

"If we love one another, God lives in us and his love is made complete in us." (1 John 4:12)

Reflection Question:

Do you see ways that your suffering is being transformed into that which brings glory to God? Where do you need to grow in God's love to more fully reflect His glory?

Strategy Recap

- ◆ **Be saturated in His presence through worship.**
- ◆ **Behold the Father through the Son.**
- ◆ **Be transformed by His love.**
- ◆ **Become His love to others.**

Training

Facilitator: Allow 15-20 minutes of quiet time for guided reflection. At the end of the reflection time, invite the group to share what God is showing them.

Beholding God

Reflect. "We become what we behold." What does this stir up for you?

Consider. What is the object of your most ardent effort, attention, pride or desire?

Is this a help or hindrance to your capacity for beholding and reflecting Jesus?

Many things can obscure or obstruct our vision and experience of the Lord. Patterns and habits that go back a long way in our life can become a hindrance to beholding—grief, unbelief, disappointment, desire for approval, idols, addictions, worldly pursuits . . . to name a few. Even *good* things—service, work, family, children, ministry, belongings, entertainment—can get in the way of the *better*. Jesus.

We are bound to what we behold. Where does God want to liberate you?

Continued on next page.

Training Continued

Ask God to show you the obstacle to your ability to clearly see, receive and reflect Christ. Allow Him to release you from that thing you are holding on to or that is holding on to you. Receive His healing grace. If there is a word or thought that comes to you, write it down. Respond to what you are hearing.

Jesus longs to dwell with us in the hospitality of an undivided heart.

Read the following passage beholding Christ in His glory.

> "Then I turned to see the voice that spoke with me. And having turned I saw seven golden lampstands, and in the midst of the seven lampstands One like the Son of Man, clothed with a garment down to the feet and girded about the chest with a golden band. His head and hair were white like wool, as white as snow, and His eyes like a flame of fire; His feet were like fine brass, as if refined in a furnace, and His voice as the sound of many waters; He had in His right hand seven stars, out of His mouth went a sharp two-edged sword, and His countenance was like the sun shining in its strength. And when I saw Him, I fell at His feet as dead. But He laid His right hand on me, saying to me, 'Do not be afraid; I am the First and the Last. I am He who lives, and was dead, and behold, I am alive forevermore. Amen.'" (Revelation 1:12-18 NKJV)

Close your eyes and contemplate Him who frees you from your sins by His blood and has made you to be His child, His priest—the apple of His eye. Behold—a door standing open in heaven! Hear His voice like a trumpet calling . . .

"Come up here, my Beloved! Come up here."

SHARE what the Lord is showing you.

Facilitator:
Close with a short prayer or the Lord's Prayer. If time permits you may pray together allowing the unit content and Training to inform your prayers. At the end of Closing Prayer, ask for a volunteer to facilitate the group if you will be having a next meeting.

Going Deeper

Going Deeper exercises are designed for use in personal quiet time with God between sessions.

◆ **Revisit** Unit 12 – Beholding God.

◆ **Repeat** the Training Exercise and any unit elements that speak to your heart.

◆ **Spend** time beholding the Father.

"The LORD bless you and keep you;
The LORD make His face shine upon you,
And be gracious to you;
The LORD lift up His countenance upon you,
And give you peace."
(Numbers 6:24-26 NKJV)

units 9-12 REVIEW & REFLECT

Facilitator:
Allow 30-40 minutes for group members to answer the Review and Reflect Questions. Invite the group to share what God has shown them.

Unit 9 – At the King's Table

Strategy Recap

- **Come with confidence to the King's Table.**
- **Be assured of the place set for you.**
- **Partake and be satisfied in His bountiful provision.**

- How is coming to the King's table bringing assurance of God's love and provision for you?

- How does this satisfy both your heart and mind?

- God's heart for you is that you shall not be in want. What is He restoring as you are seated at His table?

- How does feasting on His provision and presence change the way you see your enemies? How does it affect your prayer life?

- Do you have any personal experience with the **Going Deeper** exercise you can share?

Unit 10 – The Battle Ready Warrior

Strategy Recap

- **Recognize that there is an all-out war from the enemy on the identity, authority and purity of the name of Jesus.**
- **Recognize that there is an all-out assault by the enemy on the identity, authority, purity and destiny of God's people.**
- **Know that our God is the Lord of heaven's armies. He is the One who equips, trains and leads us into battle.**

- How have worship and stillness before God prepared you for battle?

- How has putting on the full armor of God made you more alert to the enemy's schemes?

- How has His armor prepared you to stand firm in your identity, intimacy and authority in Christ?

- Which attributes of the Battle Ready Warrior are transforming your prayer life?

- Do you have any personal experience with the **Going Deeper** exercise you can share?

Unit 11 – The Overcoming Warrior

Strategy Recap

- ◆ **Seek God's strategy for your battle.**
- ◆ **Hold your God-given position.**
- ◆ **Fix your hope on His victory, not on the rubble.**
- ◆ **Exercise the authority of His Word.**
- ◆ **Trust God to fight for you.**

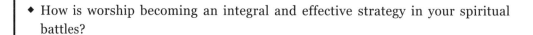

- ◆ How is worship becoming an integral and effective strategy in your spiritual battles?

- ◆ How does humility and right alignment with God position you for victory?

- ◆ Has God revealed any specific battle strategies for you to implement? Which strategies in this unit are most helpful to you at this time?

- ◆ Do you have any personal experience with the **Going Deeper** exercise you can share?

Unit 12 – Beholding God

Strategy Recap

- Be saturated in His presence through worship.
- Behold the Father through the Son.
- Be transformed by His love.
- Become His love to others.

- How do you see this ministry of beholding God active in your life?

- Are you noticing a change in your capacity to be stilled?

- Are you aware of healing that is happening as a result?

- Are you trusting God to transform your suffering into that which will bring Him glory? In what ways are you seeing this happen?

- Do you have any personal experience with the **Going Deeper** exercise you can share?

Unit 1 Additional Training
Worship, Stillness and Scripture

Lectio Divina: Abiding and Abounding in the Word

Lectio Divina is Latin for divine reading, spiritual reading, holy reading. It can also be described as holy listening.

"This is what the Sovereign Lord says: 'In repentance and rest is your salvation, in quietness and trust is your strength.'" (Isaiah 30:15)

♦ **Begin** by quieting yourself before the Lord. Be still and aware of His presence.

"I have stilled and quieted my soul; like a weaned child is my soul within me." (Psalm 131:2)

♦ **Read** Psalm 23. Try reading it aloud to engage more of your faculties in responding to the Word. *Listen* carefully. *Notice* where there is special "movement" or attraction for you in the passage. *Repeat* the passage 2 or 3 times.

♦ **Contemplate** – Consider the meaning this Word holds for you. Ask God to show you His purpose for you in it. Mull it over. Chew on it. How does it illuminate your life or present circumstance? Where does it lead or direct you?

♦ **Pray** – Share your thoughts with the Father. Listen for His words to you. This is the communion He longs for. Enjoy Him in it, even as He delights in you.

♦ **Rest** – Be still under the loving gaze of the Father. Do not try to think or pray or make anything happen. Just rest in quiet gratitude with the Word of Life, and let the Spirit deepen his work in you. Let your thoughts pass by like boats on a river and welcome the presence of Jesus.

"Be still and know that I am God." (Psalm 46:10)

Share what God is showing you.

Unit 2 Additional Training
Invitation To Relationship

For His Name's Sake

"He guides me in paths of righteousness for his names' sake." (Psalm 23:3)

Consider a pressing need or circumstance you are facing.

Ask God who He wants to be for you in this situation or relationship. How might He reveal Himself in this place that wasn't possible otherwise?

Reflect on the list of *Names of God* in Unit 2 as you converse with Him:

- What name, title or attribute stands out to you?

- How does this facet of the Father's love minister to your present need or circumstance?

- What does He want to reveal to you about His character?

- What steps might you need to take in order to allow Him access to you in this way?

- How might this bring glory and honor to His name?

Receive what He has for you with a grateful heart.

Rest in His presence.

Share what God is showing you.

Unit 3 Additional Training
Confession and Repentance

Fellowship With God

"God has now made you to share in the very life of Christ! He has forgiven you all your sins: Christ utterly wiped out the damning evidence of broken laws and commandments which always hung over our heads, and has completely annulled it by nailing it over his own head on the cross. And then, having drawn the sting of all the powers and authorities ranged against us, he exposed them, shattered, empty and defeated, in his final glorious triumphant act!" (Colossians 2:13-15 J.B. Phillips)

Consider your present relationship with God. Ask Him if there is anything hindering or interrupting your fellowship with Him.

Reflect on Colossians 3:

- Are there any places of unconfessed sin in your life?

- Are you holding on to guilt and shame regarding any previously confessed and forgiven sin?

- Is there anyone that you still need to forgive?

Submit these areas to the Father.

Release all shame and guilt. The death of Jesus has cancelled out the effect of your sinful past. You are deemed "Not Guilty" by the blood of Christ.

Ask God to help you *see* Christ as He took upon Himself all the guilt and horror of your sin.

Receive His cleansing and forgiveness.

Accept without reservation His full and complete forgiveness and love.

Embrace your cleansed and forgiven identity in Christ!

"It is finished!" (John 19:30)

Share what God is showing you.

Unit 4 Additional Training
Praying From The Inside Out

Inside Out Prayer: The Kingdom of Contrast and Paradox

Read and Reflect on 2 Corinthians 4.

The Kingdom of God is full of paradox and contrast—things that are upside down and inside out, light and dark, life and death. The world tends to emphasize the importance of outer realities, appearances and material things at the expense of those inner realities and unseen truths that take precedence in the Kingdom.

As you read this 2 Corinthians 4 passage, consider the influence of worldly culture on your ability to live inside out.

- Have your inner life and spiritual health suffered for the sake of outer appearance or service?

- Has service or ministry taken precedence over intimacy with Jesus? Spiritual growth?

- Do you take your cues from unseen realities or visible circumstances in your life?

- Do you experience freedom in cultivating your hidden life with Christ? Or do you tend to be driven by the tyranny of the urgent?

- Are there adjustments that God is inviting you to make in the way you prioritize your life in Christ?

  - **Talk** with the Father.
  - **Listen** for His leading.
  - **Write** your thoughts.

Memorize 2 Corinthians 4:16-18 and take this Word of life with you wherever you go.

  - Let it dwell in you richly and inform your inner response to your outward circumstance.
  - Pray it into the bedrock of your being and fabric of every situation you encounter.
  - Thank the Father for His gift of daily inner renewal.

Share what God is showing you.

Unit 5 Additional Training
Prayer of Rest

Tabernacling With God

"And the Word became flesh, and did tabernacle among us,
And we beheld His glory, glory as of an only begotten of a father,
Full of grace and truth." (John 1:14 Young's LT)

The Israelites wrapped themselves in prayer shawls as a reminder of the sheltering protection of our Father's unconditional love. Closeting ourselves in the covering of the prayer shawl symbolizes separation from the world, setting a mood of reverence and worship for God. The prayer shawl also serves to remind us of our identity, authority and personal holiness—that we are set apart, sanctified and made holy unto God.

Christ chose to make His dwelling, or to tabernacle, with men. Covering ourselves with a prayer shawl is symbolic of choosing to tabernacle with Him, secure in the shadow of His presence, enfolded in the arms of His everlasting mercies. It lends another dimension of intimacy to the Prayer of Rest as we come under His covering, deliberately pausing in silence to rest and receive from Him.

Ready:

- ◆ Select a shawl or scarf as your prayer shawl covering.
- ◆ Choose a word that is a favorite name or attribute of God. Some examples are *Jesus, Lord, Father, Peace, Holy, Glory, Mercy, Faith, Trust.* Return to this word as a way of refocusing when you become distracted.
- ◆ Sit comfortably with eyes closed. Focus your attention on God.
- ◆ When you become aware of thoughts intruding, let them float by like boats on a river, using your chosen word to help you return to the presence of God.

Rest:

- ◆ Focus on bringing your heart and mind to rest in alert stillness before the throne of God.
- ◆ Invite the Holy Spirit to help you stay open to the Father.
- ◆ Remain silent, releasing all distractions as you surrender to His presence.
- ◆ Respond to Jesus' invitation in Matthew 11:28 – "Come to me, all you who are weary and burdened, and I will give you rest."
- ◆ Tabernacle quietly with God for approximately 20 minutes.

Respond:

- ◆ How did you experience tabernacling with the Lord?

Share what God is showing you.

Unit 6 Additional Training
Recognizing the Voice of God

Noticing God

Each day God is constantly speaking to us in many different ways to give direction, correction, affirmation and revelation. He speaks to us in our circumstances, through people and in ordinary daily activities. He also speaks to us through nature, His Word, and His Spirit in us, to name a few examples.

Consider the past week:

- ◆ What circumstances have occurred that may have been God speaking to me?

- ◆ Has a person or persons spoken something into my life that may have been from God?

- ◆ Have I had a dream or vision that could have been God showing me direction?

- ◆ Did God interrupt my daily routine with something unusual?

- ◆ Was I moved by anything in nature that directed my attention to God?

- ◆ Did I encounter anything in God's written Word, in a sermon or in worship that felt as though He were speaking directly to me?

- ◆ Were there patterns, words, or passages of Scripture that surfaced again and again?

- ◆ Did I have experiences in which I reacted rather than responded in the Spirit?

- ◆ Were there any "coincidences" that may have been God intervening in my life?

- ◆ Are there places in my life where I am feeling uncomfortable?

- ◆ Were there any other ways God may have been speaking to me?

Reflect on what God has shown you:

- ◆ What are you discerning?

- ◆ What are you feeling?

- ◆ What are you hearing?

- ◆ Is there something God wants you to do?

- ◆ Is there something He is calling you to?

Rest with what God has revealed. Ask Him for your next step in response to His voice.

Share what God is showing you.

Unit 7 Additional Training
Stones of Remembrance

Marking The Goodness of God

Mary—the teenage, pregnant, and unwed future mother of Jesus—proclaimed, "My soul glorifies the LORD and my spirit rejoices in God my Savior." (Luke 1:46) In the middle of her seemingly dire circumstance, Mary thanked God for who He is and went on to thank Him for His mercy and goodness. She marked the places where He met her personally, as well as the places where He met the nation of Israel and those who fear Him. A grateful heart changes the atmosphere even, and especially, in times of difficulty.

Look at Mary's prayer in Luke 1:46-55 as you consider a present difficulty or hardship in your life:

+ Are you able to mark places of God's goodness in the midst of your hardship?

+ Can you think of things surrounding your difficulty that are true, noble, right, pure, lovely, admirable, excellent or praiseworthy (Philippians 4:8)?

+ Do you see evidence of God's hand of deliverance in your present situation?

+ Ponder these things! (Philippians 4:8)

Write a prayer of thanks or make a list of those things that elicit a thankful response in the midst of this hardship:

Reflect:

+ Do you notice any shift in your experience of this hardship or difficulty? If so, how?

+ If not, stay with this strategy for a while, trusting God to renovate your response.

Share what God is showing you.

Unit 8 Additional Training
Praying Like The Bride, Not The Widow

Chosen – Cherished – Beloved of Christ...

This is who Jesus says you are. Where is your identity at odds with the Bride of Christ?

Read the following Scripture as if Jesus is speaking to you. Stay as long as it takes to hear His word to you.

"Enlarge the place of your tent, stretch your tent curtains wide, do not hold back; lengthen your cords, strengthen your stakes. For you will spread out to the right and to the left; your descendants will dispossess nations and settle in their desolate cities. Do not be afraid; you will not be put to shame. Do not fear disgrace; you will not be humiliated. You will forget the shame of your youth and remember no more the reproach of your widowhood. For your Maker is your husband—the LORD Almighty is his name—the Holy One of Israel is your Redeemer; he is called the God of all the earth." (Isaiah 54:2-5)

Remember, the widow and the Bride describe the condition of our hearts in relationship to Jesus, not gender or marital status.

What are the areas of sin, shame, disgrace or iniquity that God wants to peel away?
List those things that come to mind.

Ask God to show you the wardrobe of righteousness Jesus is offering you to replace those grave clothes. Strategy: look for the opposite. List those characteristics that come to mind.

Example: *Unloved*   *Beloved*

Deliberately, intentionally, prayerfully—take off the old and put on the new Bride clothes Jesus has for you.

Acknowledge the unbreakable covenant of love Christ has for you.

Share what God is showing you.

Unit 9 Additional Training
At The King's Table

Hidden Manna and a White Stone

Jesus said, "To those who overcome I will give some of the hidden manna and a white stone with a new name known only to the one who receives it." (Revelation 2:17) This is the present-future reality of believers in the world today who press through trying times and circumstances to partake of God's hidden manna—the spiritual provision, revelation and sustenance we have in Jesus Christ, the Bread of Life. And what of the white stone?

In ancient times, it was traditional to offer honored guests a white stone with a secret name or message for their eyes only. Olympic athletes were awarded white stones inscribed with their personal achievement and prize. The stone was also used as a token giving its bearer access to special events, celebrations and feasts. For Christians, the white stone is our place holder at His Kingdom table that identifies us as His own, carrying attributes and authority belonging to Christ.

The wedding banquet is ready! The King awaits your presence.

Reflect on the significance of the hidden manna and the white stone Jesus promises His overcomers.

♦ Have you received your place at His table?

♦ Are you partaking of the hidden manna?

♦ Imagine the white stone. What has He inscribed upon it in His own hand?

God is present-future in His unfailing provision to us. While this feast and identification will reach their fullness at the wedding celebration of the Lamb, we partake by faith of the bread and the cup of Christ in the here and now.

Share what God is showing you.

Unit 10 Additional Training
The Battle Ready Warrior

Assessing Battle Readiness

"Many are the afflictions of the righteous, but the LORD delivers him out of them all."
(Psalm 34:19 NKJV)

The heart of the Battle Ready Warrior is steadfast. He is undaunted by danger and unfazed by adversity because of his unshakeable confidence in the goodness of God. He dares to trust his heavenly Father with every circumstance, knowing God's grace is more than sufficient to meet every need.

Consider these words to the Battle Ready Warrior:

"Dear friends, do not be surprised at the painful trial you are suffering, as though something strange were happening to you. But rejoice that you participate in the sufferings of Christ, so that you may be overjoyed when his glory is revealed." (1 Peter 4:12-13)

"Praise be to the God and Father of our Lord Jesus Christ! In his great mercy he has given us new birth into a living hope through the resurrection of Jesus Christ from the dead, and into an inheritance that can never perish, spoil or fade—kept in heaven for you, who through faith are shielded by God's power until the coming of the salvation that is ready to be revealed in the last time. In this you greatly rejoice, though now for a little while you may have had to suffer grief in all kinds of trials. These have come so that your faith—of greater worth than gold, which perishes even though refined by fire—may be proved genuine and may result in praise, glory and honor when Jesus Christ is revealed." (1 Peter 1:3-7)

- What is your usual attitude toward trials and adversity that arise in your life?

- How do trying circumstances affect your view and experience of God?

- Underline any words or verses that catch your attention. Consider why they might be important.

- What principles stand out for you as key to your preparation as the Battle Ready Warrior?

- How would you gauge your confidence in the unfailing love, goodness and provision of your Heavenly Father to protect you through any and all adversity?

- Do you need a faith upgrade to be battle-ready? Talk with the Father about this.

Share what God is showing you.

Unit 11 Additional Training
The Overcoming Warrior

Declaring God's Word For Personal Needs and Kingdom Gatekeeping

The Lord, as King of the Universe, issues His decrees. For example, "I will be your God and you will be my people."

Decree – Royal authority; a course of action authoritatively determined; authority; legal standing.

We have the authority to declare His decrees aloud. There is power and authority in speaking His truth and promises into specific needs or situations. His Word is so much more powerful than our own words.

Declare – Speak forth; proclaim; in Hebrew—to purchase, to buy, own.

"I will declare the decree: The LORD has said to Me,
'You are My Son, today I have begotten You.'" (Psalm 2:7 NKJV)

Some guidelines for making declarations:

- ◆ Confession and repentance is the vital first step in preparation.
- ◆ Follow that by putting on the full armor of God—see Unit 10.
- ◆ The blood of Jesus is our covering. The name of Jesus is our authority.
- ◆ Whatever you declare must line up with the Word of God. For example, you cannot declare that you will win the lottery because that is not found in Scripture.
- ◆ Godly declaration requires us to shift from saying, "Lord, would you be my rock?" to "Lord, you are my rock."
- ◆ If you are at a loss for where to begin, declare your identity in Christ—see Unit 2.
- ◆ When in doubt, it is always helpful to pray the "instead ofs" in Isaiah 61—"the oil of gladness instead of mourning, a garment of praise instead of a spirit of despair."
- ◆ This is Bridal prayer—see Unit 8.
- ◆ Be aware that the enemy does not like this kind of prayer.

Continued on next page.

Unit 11 Additional Training
The Overcoming Warrior (Continued)

DECLARATION FOR PERSONAL NEED

Consider

- What is a current personal prayer need?

- Ask God to help you find a Scripture to declare over your situation.

KINGDOM GATEKEEPING

Each of us has a position and place in the Kingdom of God. If we do not know our position and place, we cannot do the work God has purposed for us to do. These assignments are sometimes referred to as "gatekeeping."

"In keeping with the ordinance of his father David, he appointed the divisions of the priests for their duties, and the Levites to lead the praise and to assist the priests according to each day's requirement. He also appointed the gatekeepers by divisions for the various gates, because this was what David the man of God had ordered." (2 Chronicles 8:14)

Consider

- Do you know what assignment (gate to keep) you have been given for Kingdom prayer?

- Ask God to help you find a Scripture to declare over the gate you are keeping.

Share what God is showing you.

Going Deeper: Declare God's Word Into Your Home
Read aloud through a portion of Scripture as you stand in each of the four corners in every room of your house. For example, read through the Book of Colossians as you move from room to room.

Unit 12 Additional Training
Beholding God

Come Up Here, My Beloved

Reflect. "We become what we behold."

Consider. What consumes most of your energy or attention? Is this a help or hindrance to your capacity for beholding and reflecting Jesus?

Many things can obscure or obstruct our vision and experience of the Lord. Patterns and habits that go back a long way in our life can become a hindrance to beholding—grief, unbelief, disappointment, desire for approval, idols, addictions, worldly pursuits . . . to name a few. Even *good* things—service, work, family, children, ministry, belongings, entertainment—can get in the way of the *better*. Jesus.

We are bound to what we behold. Where does God want to liberate you?

Ask God to show you the obstacle to your ability to clearly see, receive and reflect Christ. Allow Him to enable you to release that thing you are holding on to or that is holding on to you. Receive His healing grace. If there is a word or thought that comes to you, write it down. Respond to what you are hearing.

Jesus longs to dwell with us in the hospitality of an undivided heart. Read the following passage beholding Christ in His glory.

> "As I looked, thrones were set in place, and the Ancient of Days took his seat.
> His clothing was as white as snow; the hair of his head was white like wool.
> His throne was flaming with fire, and its wheels were all ablaze.
> A river of fire was flowing, coming out from before him.
> Thousands upon thousands attended him; ten thousand times ten thousand stood before him.
> The court was seated, and the books were opened. . . .
> In my vision at night I looked, and there before me was one like a son of man, coming with the clouds
> of heaven. He approached the Ancient of Days and was led into his presence. He was given authority,
> glory and sovereign power; all nations and peoples of every language worshiped him. His dominion is an
> everlasting dominion that will not pass away, and his kingdom is one that will never be destroyed."
> (Daniel 7:9,10,13,14)

Close your eyes and contemplate Him who frees you from your sins by His blood and has made you to be His child and priest to serve Him. . . the very apple of His eye. Behold—a door standing open in heaven! Hear His voice like a trumpet calling. . .

"Come up here, my Beloved! Come up here."

Share what the Lord is showing you.

SCRIPTURE INDEX

SCRIPTURE INDEX

SCRIPTURE INDEX

Ordering *Prayer Boot Camp*

To order *Prayer Boot Camp* or contact Hidden Manna Ministry, please visit our website at **www.HiddenMannaMinistry.com**. **Click** on **HMM Store**.

Workbook Pricing:

Individual rate (1-9 copies)	$15 each
Small Group rate (10 or more copies)	$12.50 each
Community rate (25 or more copies)	$11 each
Tax & Shipping additional	

Mailing address:

Hidden Manna Ministry, PO Box 928, Somis, CA 93066

Sound the Shofar!
Awaken from your slumber.
Arise from your sleep.
It is time, my Beloved.

Fear not.
Draw near.
Receive my love for you.

Stand on my Word – it is life and strength to you.
Lift your voice.
Declare my goodness and my glory.
I have made you and prepared you for such a time as this.